"Together Live is a storyt _____ ___ series featuring an inspiring array of participants from comedian Cameron Esposito to writers Ashley C. Ford and Sue Monk Kidd. And now essays from four years of touring are collected in *Hungry Hearts,* edited by Jennifer Rudolph Walsh. You'll find kindred spirits in these tales of resilience, transformation, and joy."

—*Time*

"Sue Monk Kidd! Ashley C. Ford! Cameron Esposito! Bozoma Saint John! The gang's all here—in this book of essays, 16 writers reflect movingly on all different ways to be in loving relationships. If you are looking for a little bit of gentleness, a warm word from writers you can trust, well, here it is."

—*Glamour*

"Unlike many women's conferences, Together Live is not about a work-life balance or having it all, but rather focused on convening women across diverse backgrounds and generations to share their raw stories, build community, take action, and find self-love."

—*Bustle*

"Walsh has turned her love for storytelling into a live event where women of all backgrounds can come together to share their unique stories. . . . Together Live encompasses Walsh's forte of sharing powerful stories with celebrating and honoring the diverse group of women that come together."

—*Forbes*

HUNGRY HEARTS

HUNGRY HEARTS

ESSAYS ON COURAGE, DESIRE, AND BELONGING

EDITED BY **JENNIFER RUDOLPH WALSH**

FEATURING ESSAYS BY
★ LUVVIE AJAYI JONES ★ AMENA BROWN ★
★ AUSTIN CHANNING BROWN ★
★ CAMERON ESPOSITO ★ ASHLEY C. FORD ★
★ NATALIE GUERRERO ★ SUE MONK KIDD ★
★ CONNIE LIM (MILCK) ★ NKOSINGIPHILE MABASO ★
★ JILLIAN MERCADO ★ PRIYA PARKER ★
★ GEENA ROCERO ★ BOZOMA SAINT JOHN ★
★ TANYA BLOUNT-TROTTER ★ MICHAEL TROTTER JR. ★
★ MAYSOON ZAYID ★

THE DIAL PRESS
NEW YORK

2022 Dial Press Trade Paperback Edition

Published in the United States by The Dial Press, an imprint of Random House, a division of Penguin Random House LLC, New York.

THE DIAL PRESS is a registered trademark and the colophon is a trademark of Penguin Random House LLC.

Originally published in hardcover in the United States by The Dial Press, an imprint of Random House, a division of Penguin Random House LLC, in 2021.

LIBRARY OF CONGRESS CATALOGING-IN-PUBLICATION DATA
Names: Walsh, Jennifer Rudolph, editor.
Title: Hungry hearts: essays on courage, desire, and belonging / edited by Jennifer Rudolph Walsh.
Description: First edition. | New York: The Dial Press, [2021]
Identifiers: LCCN 2020053309 (print) | LCCN 2020053310 (ebook) | ISBN 97805932229637 (paperback) | ISBN 9780593229644 (ebook)
Subjects: LCSH: American essays—Women authors. | American essays—21st century. | Women authors, American—Biography. | Love. | Self. | Belonging (Social psychology) | Resilience (Personality trait)
Classification: LCC PS683.W65 H86 2021 (print) | LLC PS683.W65 (ebook) | DDC 814/.60809287—d23
LC record available at https://lccn.loc.gov/2020053309
LC ebook record available at https://lccn.loc.gov/2020053310

Printed in the United States of America on acid-free paper

randomhousebooks.com

1st Printing

*For my mother, Stephanie, in all her phases—
the four-year-old child who lost her mommy,
the young woman searching for love,
the single mom finding her way in the world,
the Bubbe who finally found belonging and joy.
Even though you don't see what a mighty story you carry,
it's your courage and resilience that created my
lifelong love affair with storytelling.*

CONTENTS

CONTENTS

INTRODUCTION

JENNIFER RUDOLPH WALSH

IF I TOLD YOU THAT MY PARENTS GOT DIVORCED when I was nine years old, it would communicate a fact—but it wouldn't help you know me better. What if, instead, I told you this: One morning when I was nine years old, my dad told us we were having a family meeting after school. I was so excited, I could barely breathe. I had never been to a meeting before and it sounded important. Between classes, I asked some friends if they'd ever been to one, and my friend Pamela explained to me that a family meeting is when you decide where you are going on vacation. *Wow!* I thought. *My first vacation!* She told me about an amazing ride at Disney World called It's a Small World and sang me the song about a small world with a shared sun, where a smile meant friendship to everyone. It sounded like heaven.

When I got home from school, I found a yellow legal pad and wrote a detailed list of the reasons Disney World was an educational place. I arrived at our family meeting ready to advocate for my choice with all my might. When, instead of calling the meeting to order and asking where we'd like to go on vacation, my parents calmly sat down and told my siblings and me that they were getting divorced, my mind went blank. All I can remember now is how desperately I hugged the legal pad to my chest, wishing I could make it disappear. I had never been so wrong about something so big. That moment was a tectonic shift not only in my understanding of my family, but in the way I trusted myself and the world. What else did I think was permanent that might change in an instant? How else was my innocence leaving me exposed to pain and confusion? I can still feel the legal pad's solid edges pressing into my hands—the physical, almost shameful evidence of a world I no longer inhabited and never would again.

I expose my vulnerability by telling you about my Disney World list instead of just saying "When I was nine my parents got divorced" because I want to share more of myself—my history, my soul, my heart. And I believe that sharing my full humanity honors you, in your full humanity. After a lifetime of listening and thirty years working as a literary agent, professionally midwifing thousands of people's stories, I've learned firsthand that bravely sharing our truth and encouraging others to share theirs creates a type of magic that has the power to heal and connect us more deeply to one another.

Sharing our authentic stories can be transformational. Someone may look very different from us on the outside, but what our true stories reveal is that, on the inside, we have all experienced similar feelings of heartbreak, failure, betrayal, longing, triumph, and joy. We all want the same things—to be loved, to be seen, and to belong. We all have dreams that our lives will make a difference. Our stories illustrate that.

It's all too easy to compare our insides to other people's outsides, imagining some version of a perfect life others are living, while we are left with our imperfect ones. In that disconnect between our perception and reality is a void where loneliness, anxiety, and depression often grow. But there is an antidote—one we all have access to. Sharing the real stories of our hearts, our vulnerable and hungry hearts, allows us to connect to others—*insides to insides*. When someone hears our story, we feel seen, we know we matter, and we instantly realize we're not alone. That's why I call it magic. Because it is.

My purpose has always been to amplify people's voices, to build a giant megaphone for people to be heard far and wide. "This book will change everything" is something I have said and meant too many times to count. Great books are like that—totally transformational. I cannot imagine where I would be had I not been found—like a search and rescue team locating me on a snowy mountain—by books. Growing up, Maya Angelou, Toni Morrison, Alice Walker, and Maxine Hong Kingston were my most impactful teachers. Finding me in my lonely teenage bedroom, they shined a light, gave me words for my own experience, and made me feel I belonged. It made perfect sense that I would want to spend my adult life as close to books and their authors as possible.

After two decades as the leader of the literary division of a major global talent agency, representing and advocating for the most amazing, courageous, trailblazing, and luminous authors on the planet, selling their books to publishers and filmmakers and bringing their words into the world, living my dream come true every day, something unexpected happened: my dream evolved.

Authors write in solitude and we read in solitude. I've always loved that—but I found myself starting to long for community in a more intimate and immediate way. I wanted to bring people together as stories were shared, craving the magnified power of a collective experience. The universe provided the most perfect opportunity, and I was beyond blessed to collaborate on Oprah Winfrey's The Life You Want tour. I spent twelve weeks on the road with hundreds of thousands of people, forming a collective heartbeat of hope and change. I joked it should have been called "the life *I* want" tour because I never wanted it to end. But when it did, I knew there was no going back for me. Something too big had shifted inside me.

I yearned to turn up the volume on the voices our mainstream media culture wasn't often giving the microphone to: people of color, LGBTQIA+ people, disabled people, and people of all religious faiths. Out of that yearning, Together Live was born.

A speaking tour featuring the storytelling of writers, poets, musicians, and performers of all sorts, Together Live aimed to share stories from a stage that featured a diverse group of people, mostly womxn and the occasional man, who shared a desire for a more compassionate, equal, and just world. We made sure that ticket prices were affordable so that everyone with a hungry heart would be welcome. We set sail in the fall of 2016, and for four years our traveling love rally, including the contributors in this anthology, communed with fifty thousand kindred spirits. The word most often used to describe our event was "life-changing." *Life-changing.* Yet all we did was sit on a couch onstage, share our wholehearted truths, and ask the audience to do the same. We entered every night as strangers in a new city and ended every night as a family—dancing, laughing, and crying together.

When it became clear that we would not be able to

gather in theaters around the country in 2020, many of the outrageously talented and generous souls who had participated in Together Live decided to share their stories in book form. This anthology is the result of this effort. The title, *Hungry Hearts,* came from Sue Monk Kidd's essay "Women on the Loose," in which she describes a "big hungry thing in [her] heart" that was pushing her to write, when she "knew nothing about being a writer." Reading Sue's brilliant words, I wondered: What do our deepest hearts' desires say about who we are? What does the hunger in our hearts motivate us to do? When we listen to what our hearts have to say, what do we hear? The incredible essays in this collection offer a range of answers to these questions. This anthology features the work of an intersectional group of storytellers writing with their own unique perspectives, yet all sharing a desire to find purpose, community, and resilience in the face of heartbreak, discomfort, and fear. As a group, these contributors are wildly diverse, yet they all have a brave and compassionate open heart. And on our Together Live tour, despite our many differences and varied lived experiences, we became a "road family." Turns out that Disney World ride was right, it is a small world after all.

As a culture, we've learned a lot about division, loss, and change. Yet when all else falls away, we have our stories and we have one another. Full stop. My hope is that as you read each person's vulnerable truth, you'll be given courage to share your own. As you remember the confusion, shame, and fear of a moment when, unsuspectingly, your world turned upside down, like it did for me with my yellow legal pad pressed to my chest, you will take a chance and share it, perhaps with someone who looks nothing like you. You'll see first-hand what I mean by magic. I believe in my bones that authentic storytelling is a radical act of love that can connect and heal our fractured world. For it to work, we need your story too. Together, we rise.

HUNGRY HEARTS

WOMEN ON THE LOOSE

SUE MONK KIDD

I ONCE STENCILED SOME WORDS ON A WALL IN MY house. At the top of the stairs, where you couldn't possibly miss it, I painted a quotation by French novelist Emile Zola: "If you ask me what I came to do in this world, I, an artist, will answer you, 'I am here to live out loud.'"

Every day I would pause and read the words and try to take them in. What did it mean to live out loud? Did I have the courage? If so, what sort of reverberation did I hope to make out there in the world?

One day, as I read the quotation for at least the hundredth time, instead of the word *artist,* I spontaneously, without reason or forethought, substituted the word *woman:* I, a *woman,* will answer you, "I am here to live out loud." I stood there a moment, the tiniest bit electrified, as the words seemed to do a double flip off the wall. Imagine: women—not just artists or people with public platforms—but women, all of us, living out loud!

Today, that vision is becoming increasingly realized, and yet women still remain the largest untapped resource on the planet. It's never been more apparent to me that the plights and problems in our world cannot be solved without the power and presence of the Feminine. Women's out-loudness is more than an alluring vision. It's an indispensable ethic.

LONG AGO, I was a thirty-year-old with two toddlers, a little brick house, a husband, a dog, and a big, untamed yearning lodged in the center of my chest. I wanted to write words that would find their way into the world. I had a degree in nursing. I knew nothing about being a writer, the craft of writing, or where to begin. All I had was the big hungry thing in my heart.

And fear. I had a lot of that. What if I couldn't do it? What if I fell flat on my face? What if . . . what if? I finally got sick of hearing myself. I have a postcard that sits on my desk with a quotation by Charlotte Brontë: "I'm just going to write because I cannot help it." I made my way to the edge of becoming—to that place where the desire to pursue one's passion becomes greater than one's fear of failure—because I couldn't help myself.

Leaping was involved, as when the trapeze artist turns herself loose of her trapeze bar and pivots, turning in midair, suspended on nothing but her own audacity, and reaches out for the bar she hopes is swinging toward her. I don't know why writing words and sending them into the world felt like I was risking my neck, but that's how it was. When it comes to outloudness, that's often the case.

I had to face down insidious voices in my head that told me I shouldn't write because it was too big a risk, because I already had a perfectly good career, plus when would I have time? Besides, I couldn't do it because I had no MFA or experience and most everyone thought it was an outlandish enterprise. There they were, the sinister twins—Don't and Can't. I patched together my courage. I took a hundred deep breaths. I told myself: If you're going to err, Sue, you might as well do it on the side of audacity.

The poet David Whyte wrote a line that feels deeply true to me: "Revelation must be terrible knowing you can never hide your voice again." Living out loud is both terrible and beautiful. It's terrible because there's a vulnerability to it. It's beautiful because there's a vulnerability to it. It's much safer and nicer and innocuous to remain unseen and silent. But in this way we close ourselves off from the world, and possibly from our own deep selves.

As a novice, Twyla Tharp, the great American dancer and choreographer, was stymied when faced with composing one of her earliest dances, so she stood on the stage, stamped her foot, and shouted, "Begin!" To this day, that's how her dance "The Fugue" starts, with the stamp of a foot. She wrote, "Just begin and worry about the consequences later."

I simply began.

I realized I just wanted to write because I cannot help it. Please, substitute anything you would like for the word *write*. It could be: I just want to start a book club at a women's shelter because I cannot help it. I just want to teach girls self-esteem because I cannot help it. I just want collect bottle caps and make art with them . . . I just want to create a dream group . . . I just want to march for racial justice . . . I just want to play the cello . . . I just want to run for Congress . . . I just want to promote sustainable food programs . . . I just want to sew bibs for baby girls that say "When I grow up I want to be president." (That latter want-to belongs to my ninety-eight-year-old mother.) There are as many possibilities to live out loud as there are people. They are all deserving of a chance.

★ ★
★

LIVING OUT LOUD doesn't mean you go out there and make noise, any noise. It means expressing the genuine sound in your heart. I'm of the opinion that every woman possesses a capacity, a passion, or a spark that's meant not only for herself but for the world around her as well. I like to call this spark her particular genius.

What if genius isn't rare but accessible? Merriam-Webster defines genius as: "1. a person who has a level of talent or intelligence that is very rare or remarkable; 2. a person who is very good at doing something; 3. great natural ability."

We've come to identify genius almost exclusively with the first definition. Most people seem to think it belongs to a small, elite group of men. The Einsteins, the Mozarts. I stumbled upon a list on the internet titled the "Top 50 Geniuses of All Time." The first time I read it, I found no women. That couldn't be right. I read it again. Still no women. I tried another list labeled "Greatest Minds of All Time," which ranked one hundred geniuses. Marie Curie made it. One woman, ninety-nine men.

If you want to find women geniuses on the internet, it helps to search "*women* geniuses." Apparently there are geniuses and then there are women geniuses. I speculated that maybe I was being overly sensitive, but when I typed "women genius" into the search bar, I was prompted: "Did you mean women genius or Female Genius band?" I persisted—yes, I actually meant "women genius." Then a little box popped up and I was informed that people who search for "women geniuses" also search for "smart blond actresses." You would think I'm making this up, but I swear the truth of it on my dog's life. Still, I persisted, and it turns out there are so many geniuses of the female persuasion in the history of the world, I thought my heart would crack open with the joy of reading their names. Some names I'd never before heard. Names I should have heard.

I'm for demystifying the word *genius,* for making it user-friendly. Therefore, let's go with the second aspect of the definition: a person who is very good at doing something.

We each have a particular genius. The late novelist John Gardner called it our "necessary fire." It's an energy that lives within us at the intersection of imagination and feeling. The quest to discover it, and sometimes to rediscover it, often begins by noticing the places of combustion in our life, by simply observing what brings us alive, by paying attention to what fascinates us. The soul lures us through aliveness and fascination.

Sometimes, though, our particular genius is so hidden, forgotten, caged, shy, camouflaged, or neglected, it's tempting to declare ourselves devoid of it. One way we know it's there is through the restlessness it gives off.

Somewhere in my mid-forties, after more than a dozen years of writing memoir and nonfiction, I became restless. It was a vague feeling that seemed connected to my writing. During that strange, fidgety interlude, I traveled to Crete with a group of women, and while there we visited an ancient convent. In the center of the convent's courtyard stood a centuries-old myrtle tree with a Black Madonna icon perched in its serpentine branches. A Greek Orthodox nun invited us to participate in a tradition of stepping beneath the branches and asking for "what lies at the bottom of our hearts."

What lay at the bottom of my heart? I was sure I didn't know, but as I stepped beneath the canopy of branches, I heard myself mutter, "I would like to become a novelist." Somewhere inside I knew this about myself, but I'd never articulated it.

Now and then we have to ask the "bottom of the heart" question and see what wiggles to the surface. Occasionally we need to coax our particular genius to show itself.

By the time I returned home from Crete, my restlessness had been replaced with a sense of direction. *I just want to write a novel because I can't help myself.*

Once again, I was a beginner, trying to find my way toward becoming good at something.

* * *

IN MY BOOK *The Dance of the Dissident Daughter,* I tell the story of thirty-five Norwegian women known as the *kjerringsleppet,* a word that roughly translates as "women on the loose." The group formed back in 1989 after women were excluded from participating in the opening ceremony of Norway's Alpine Center. Because only men were invited to ski ceremoniously down the slope, the thirty-five women banded together and waited in the woods until the appropriate moment, then shocked everyone by swooping out of the trees on their skis, clanging cowbells and crashing the ceremony. Norway loved it. The women even became a fond symbol, so much so that they were invited to open the giant slalom competition at the 1994 Winter Olympics in Lillehammer. The women on the loose had a motto: Improvise, surprise, and come uninvited.

When I think of women living out loud, I think of these women. Their out-loudness changed a set of beliefs about gender inclusion.

I've carried this vision with me for a long time now: Women ringing their big feminine cowbells. Women on the loose. Women imparting their genius to a world desperately in need of it.

We're just going to do it because we cannot help it.

REACHING FOR AMBITION

AUSTIN CHANNING BROWN

A BLACK PERFORMING ARTS SCHOOL WAS MY INTRO-duction to theater. I held tight to my mother's hand as we weaved around excited teenagers and proud parents to find our seats. Music that had been bursting from the speakers suddenly stopped. The lights lowered in the high school gymnasium. Plastic folding chairs scraped across the floor as the audience settled in. Spotlights circled before landing on the center of the stage where a Black Peter Pan stood, hands on hips, green hat tilted to the side. For an hour and a half, I sat entranced at the spectacle: props, costumes, and the prettiest Tinker Bell I'd ever seen. I was just a small kid, easily dropped into the story unfolding before me.

At the end of the play, my mother and I leapt up, moving toward the stage, hoping to congratulate my grandmother. She was a home economics teacher at the high school, and she'd been responsible for the costumes. My grandmother was always working on paintings or other artistic projects, but I couldn't believe how much she'd created for this play, from the giant props to the intricate costumes for all the main characters. Once we found her and exchanged hugs, she said there was something special she wanted me to see. Suddenly the crocodile from the play came slithering down the middle of the aisle right toward me. My heart beat fast. "What do you think?" she asked. I giggled, not taking my eyes off it. I knew it was pretend. I knew my grandmother had created this green monster. But it was so realistic. My eyes widened as I heard the *tick-tock, tick-tock, tick-tock* from the belly of the beast before me. I wanted to reach out and touch it, but, caught between wonder and suspicion, my fear screamed, "Do not get too close to the crocodile. You saw what happened to Hook!"

The sensation was thrilling: knowing in my head that I was safe, while being unable to turn off the unique mix of excitement and fear coursing through my body. I was utterly intrigued by this feeling of riskiness, where there seemed to be the potential for something exhilarating on the other side. It's the first time I remember feeling this, the tension between the two sides of risk and reward seemingly echoed by the tick-tock of the crocodile's belly, but it's far from the last.

As a writer, I know I'm safe when I sit down in front of a blank page, but I feel a thrill run through me as I consider my task: hoping my words will challenge and inspire readers, while knowing that will require vulnerability and courage on my end first.

All I knew at that moment was that the next time someone asked me "What do you want to be when you grow up?" artist would be at the top of my list.

And I had a list. I was going to be a teacher and artist, like my grandmother. I was going to adopt all kids without a home. On the side, I would sing like my pretend auntie Whitney Houston. As I grew older, it became increasingly clear that I was not in fact going to sing like Whitney, and my inability to sew, paint, or draw meant my options for artistry were far more limited than my grandmother's, but I was consistently intrigued by the idea of helping others as a career. By high school, my list included becoming a minister and working in the nonprofit sector on behalf of kids in foster care.

Despite my grand plans to change the world, I had one problem: myself. I was absolutely incapable of finishing a project. I did great in school with its deadlines and grades and clear finish lines. But entering adulthood was . . . different. While completing a degree program in Detroit, I fell in love with the city. It bothered me that though so few people understood the history of Detroit, everyone had an opinion about its decline and potential for recovery. I planned an entire curriculum on Detroit history and what it means to be a good citizen, but I never taught it. I didn't have a plan for where I would teach it. I hadn't been hired anywhere. I just felt compelled to create the curriculum and figure out the rest later.

I filled out applications for organizing and activism, but I never turned them in to the folks running the organization. I believed in the cause of racial justice but was terrified I didn't have the skills it takes to organize people. I would join a church in order to start my ministry and then would have to move following jobs wherever they landed, leaving all my plans behind. I was filled with great ideas. So many ideas. It got so bad that my husband would laugh every time I asked him excitedly, "Want to hear about my new project?" He knew I meant well. He knew it would be a good idea. And he also knew it was highly unlikely that I would follow through. I was a chronic idea generator, but once the thrill of the new idea disappeared, so did my follow-through.

I figured there must be something wrong with me. I was like my grandmother in so many ways. I wanted to create. I wanted to teach. I wanted to inspire. But unlike her, something in me must have been broken. Because she figured out how to do all of those things. I was like a chicken, flapping my wings but never flying. In my early twenties, I began to question all my child-like wonder about careers and changing the world. Maybe those were just the dreams of a kid. Maybe it was time to grow up, bury my sense of idealism, and find contentment in whatever job was paying.

In the midst of all this questioning came the Great Recession. One year into marriage and having just completed my degree, we were broke. Broke broke. So many of my grand ideas died a terrible death during the recession. But it wasn't just the ideas that took a nosedive. It was my belief that I could impact anything, let alone the world. My whole world became about survival: How would we pay our rent? Did we need to move in with our parents? Where could we find jobs? Everything felt uncertain, and that uncertainty bled into my bones. I was no longer sure about my path or purpose. Everything became about the next paycheck.

With assistance from our parents, we moved to a larger city. Secured new jobs. Did our best to ride out the remainder of the recession. But all was not well with the world. The racial tensions in America were starting to heat up again and soon boiled into an era known as Black Lives Matter.

"You must start writing," my friends encouraged me. But I shrugged it off. Working at a church, I had a small but mighty community of people who were engaged in conversations about racial justice, and I thought that was enough. We were having fun discussing the news, reading books together, and talking through justice issues with anyone who would listen. We even started a little class for congregation members to come learn about racial justice. As they watched my whole body light up while teaching, they insisted I could do more. But my hope had already died. This was enough, I told them. I'd only just gotten some stability. Why would I take a risk now, of all times? Especially knowing I probably wouldn't even follow through? But no matter what I told myself, I couldn't completely silence the tick-tock of the croc. Could they be right? I asked myself. Could there be more for me?

Eventually my friends had had enough of my avoidance. They believed when I was too scared to believe. But they did more than believe. Jenny found a website for my blog, gave me a theme, and told me she expected my first post to be up by MLK weekend. Becky scolded me for not having a social media account so that she could share what I was writing. Brenda took me to her publishing house, let me meet with her editor. When I lost my job, instead of expecting me to find another right away, my husband told me to just focus on writing for a while. And I did. I fell in love with writing. For the first time, I followed through on a project, and it felt so natural to keep going.

I have little doubt that the missing ingredient from all my projects before was community. I wanted to teach, but didn't have a classroom. I wanted to be a part of an organization, but never took the final step to join. I wanted to belong to a worship community, but became discouraged when I had to move. Every time I tried to start a new project, I had the emotional support of those around me, but I never invested in the community it takes to make dreams a reality. Turned out that even though writing is considered very isolating—just me and the page—this was the first time I was starting a project with people. I needed conversation partners and editors. I needed friends who would critique my sentences and make them better. I needed mentors to walk me through the writing process and people who would remind me of tiny details from our shared history. I suddenly had resources, guidance, advice, and my little community of readers. I had poked the crocodile. I was on my way.

Before I knew it, I had been writing consistently for four years—the most follow-through I had ever displayed on a project. I had no expectation that my blog would lead anywhere. The blog *was* the whole project. So when it led to a book deal, I couldn't believe it.

"I know I have more project ideas than a caterpillar has legs," I told my husband. "Thank you for supporting me in this."

"Of course, babe," he replied. "I have always known and loved how ambitious you are."

Record scratch.

Ambitious?

Was I ambitious?

I had never thought of myself as ambitious. Wasn't that the word to describe my brother, the software engineer? Wasn't that the word to describe my husband, the attorney? That was not the word to describe a Black woman who has a degree in social justice, was it?

Creative. Energetic. Spunky. These were all words I was familiar with—words that I'd heard used to describe women who wanted to make an impact on society, like me.

But ambition? As with the green crocodile crawling toward me as a child, I wasn't sure I could fully embrace it, but I liked the thrill of it.

I kept writing even as life continued to unfold. Packing. Moving. New jobs. Big decisions. Writing was my constant. On the blog. On social media. On the first draft of my book. Writing kept me company. But I was carefully managing my own expectations. Don't hope for too much. Let yourself be surprised if something nice happens. This right here is great. Let's not rock the boat by wanting more.

I wonder if you've sometimes felt that way. Girl meets dream. Life crushes dream. Friends revive dream. Girl holds on for dear life. That was me. I was proud of myself and grateful to my community for helping me follow through. But this word, *ambition,* felt like a truth I wasn't ready to own. I was still being revived. I loved writing. I was proud of what I had written. But I did want more. I wanted to write not just one book but as many as the publishing industry would allow. I loved teaching my little class, but was it safe to dream about bigger classrooms or larger audiences? Was it safe to hope for more beyond what I had already achieved? Or was it better to hold this close and not let go? I wasn't sure.

Then came Jo.

I knew Jo Saxton only through social media and her book, given to me by a colleague when I first started writing. It was called *More Than Enchanting: Breaking Through Barriers to Influence Your World.* Through that book, perhaps without knowing it, Jo had become one of my mentors. So when I discovered she was coming to town for an event, I took a chance and asked her if we could meet for just a second. She graciously agreed, and for half an hour over coffee I told her about all my inner barriers. I told her about my dreams as a child and how those dreams had been dashed in adulthood. I told her about my love for writing but confessed that it was the only thing I had done consistently. Could I even trust myself? And then there was this word: *ambition.* If I embraced this word, if I reached out and touched it, what would that mean? What if I could no longer contain myself?

Jo listened (and reacted audibly) as I poured out my heart. Then it was her turn. She sat straight up in her chair, set her coffee down, and looked me in the eyes as she said, "Austin, I am an ambitious woman." I swear there were more words that came after that, but I couldn't hear them over the sound of the chains falling off my own heart. What freedom to hear another Black woman so calmly and passionately lay claim to her own ambition. I interrupted, asking her to repeat that sentence again. She laughed and obliged, then launched into the story of her own journey. She told me about what ambitions she had next. And then she gave me an assignment.

"I want you to release survival, scarcity, and shame."

Well, damn. Thirty minutes and this gorgeous Black woman had named all the chains that I had picked up as I tried to tame my own ambitions. We had survived the recession, but I was still holding on to the notion that I could not dream because survival was priority. I had believed the lie of scarcity—that there was only so much room in the world for me, only a handful of opportunities, only a little space for my voice, only a tiny slice of success that could be mine. And so much shame. Even though my writing had led to an amazing opportunity, I still carried a great deal of shame about my inability to complete past projects. That shame made me afraid to try new things, but it also made me wonder if I could finish the opportunity right in front of me: a book. Hell, could I finish a *draft* of a book? I wasn't sure. My track record wasn't great. Survival. Scarcity. Shame.

After having a chance to take in Jo's words, I wrote

out all the reasons why I was still holding on to smallness and safety: "My independence is of comfort to
me; I find it hard to need community. . . . For my entire
life, I've been taught that women should be humble.
Can I be both ambitious and humble? . . . What if I try
this and fail? What if my voice isn't good enough?
What if my dreams have been crushed for a reason, to
keep me in this tiny, safe box?" I wrote and wrote and
wrote. When I had filled up the page, I took out a black
Sharpie and over the top of those words wrote myself a
letter:

> I am leaving behind survival, scarcity, and shame. I am
> embracing my call. I will walk in strength, sustainabil-
> ity, and strategy. I will remind myself that God de-
> lights in me, that God gave me this ambition. I will
> remember all that I want to do in the world. I will not
> wait for someone else's permission to be who God cre-
> ated me to be. I have things to say, and I will be excited
> for every opportunity I have to share.

It was the first time I used the word *ambition* to describe myself with pride. I had finally reached out for
the crocodile.

Sometimes I'm still afraid of my ambition, if I am
honest. My ambition and I are in a constant dance
with each other. I try hard to remember that I am the
lead; she is following me. My ambition makes me

hopeful for things that have not yet come into being, and this feels like an invitation to disappointment. An invitation to return to those years of uncertainty and smallness. But my ambition has also helped me discover that I can survive disappointment. Turns out that when I add my community to the mix, my ambition recovers from disappointment pretty quickly, actually. She's resilient, and relentless in her creativity, flexibility, and determination.

The problem was never that I wasn't good enough for my own ambitious dreams. It was that my dreams require community in order to become possible. I was never meant to try to reach my goals alone, just as I was never meant to try to impact the world alone. My mother and grandmother were standing right there next to me when the crocodile came slithering up the aisle. All I had to do was to look up at them and ask, "Will you help me do this? And if it doesn't go well, will you still be there?" It's vulnerable and scary, and it's taken me a lifetime of practice. But I've found it's worth it. To believe in myself—and others—enough to say: "I want this. I'm worthy of this. I need help getting there. And I believe you will be there for me whatever happens next."

MAKING ROOM

ASHLEY C. FORD

BRETT AND I DATED FROM THE TIME I WAS FOURTEEN years old until just a few months after my twentieth birthday. It was my sophomore year of college, his too, but we went to separate schools, an hour and a half apart. Back in high school, I could easily walk to his house from mine, just a few streets over and one long street down the way. My home was a hostile place, and he could get to me fast if I needed him, and that made me feel safe. My family structure had never felt emotionally safe for me, and from my freshman year of high school on, Brett had been the person I clung to for stability and consistent, reliable love and affection. It was enough that I could be silly, sad, and angry with him and he did not leave me. In fact, most of the time, he really liked me. And I liked him too. That was more than enough.

Home was where I felt most unsure how I would be received. The floor of my mother's house was littered with eggshells, and I took big steps. I heard and said things I should not have, even if they were true, and in my home, that eventually led to pain. As soon as I was old enough, I spent as little time in my mother's home as possible, preferring to spend time with my grand-mother. She was tough, but she loved me, and some-times she even listened to me.

During high school, I spent most of my free time with Brett, and despite being only six months older than I was, he parented me in many ways. He taught me how to drive, helped me get my first car, and in-sisted I apply to and attend college.

Now about eighty miles apart, we connected via phone, which had become less and less enjoyable over the two years we'd been chatting into various receivers. Most of our conversations began like we were testing the waters around the other, searching for a warm place to enter, but they usually devolved into argu-ments, and I hated myself for not being able to pin-point and fix the source of our troubles. I come from a blaming family. If something went wrong, or if some-thing made you feel bad, there was always someone to blame. If you couldn't find someone to blame outside of yourself, you were the problem, and you should punish yourself twice as hard as you would have punished an offender. I was used to being a problem. Blame was like an old coat I'd worn before, at least if you take away the warmth and fuzziness: familiar, and stitched into my badness by own hand.

One night, while my friends were downstairs celebrating a Super Bowl win for the Indianapolis Colts, Brett called. I thought he was calling about the game, but as I stood in the middle of a bedroom above them, in the dark, I found myself trying to hear Brett through his sobs.

"I'm so sorry, Ashley," he said, his voice splitting when he said my name. "I think . . . I think I'm gay." I held my breath.

When I was able to speak, I said, "Come talk to me." I needed him to drive through his pain, into the night, and say what he'd just said while standing in front of me. In my memory, I made this request with calm and perfect poise. I imagine a steady voice elegantly inviting her own destruction into her home, rather than having it kick the door down. This is not the way it happened. A quick return to a journal I kept during that time includes this recounting of my behavior: *I screamed at him, "Get here now! You can't do this to me over the phone!"*

He made the trip, but once he arrived, he couldn't say the words. Instead, we cried, held each other, had sex, and lay side by side without going to sleep. It was the closest we'd been to each other's bodies in weeks, and I cannot speak for him, but I had never felt more alone. The inside of my head spun and sputtered with all the weak hope of a broken dream. My desperation for him, for our relationship, a safe space in a life that felt like enduring chaos, ran from the deepest pools of my heart to my curling fingers, gripping the bottom of his undershirt in case he made a break for it in the night. I did not expect to be able to hold him back, but at least I'd be awake to watch him go.

He felt *away* from me even when we were as physically close as two people could be. Even though we had been physically intimate with each other for years, there had always been a noticeable distance between Brett and me, and it made me want to peer behind his eyelids when he closed them to me. I knew he was seeing and feeling things back there he didn't want to tell me, and I wanted in. I shared so much of myself, I felt I deserved to be let in. How else would I know when he inevitably changed his mind about loving me? I believed he was too good to be the thing that was wrong with us, and soon he would see it was me. I just wanted to see it coming.

My fixation on our relationship was less about whether or not I wanted to be with Brett and so much more about proving to myself the issue was my fault, and most likely always had been. I was not a child who had never been told they were loved, but I was a child who didn't recognize or receive that love unconditionally. I was watched and judged. I had always suspected I was unlovable, and assumed someday someone would admit it to my face. I believed Brett loved me enough to be kind about it when he eventually told me how terrible I was, and that was the most I hoped for.

We were kids trying to figure out how to be lovers, and the stakes were always higher than they should have been, right from the start. We dated for six years, an eternity among our peers, before he told me he was gay. That wasn't what made me angry. The thing was, I had been counting on Brett to make the life I dreamed of possible, the one I hadn't gotten in my childhood. The one I was convinced I couldn't make on my own. It wasn't that he was gay. I didn't think there was anything wrong with being gay. It's that being gay meant he couldn't be with me.

When he left the next morning, we hadn't decided on any specific course of action, but my heart began to accept that we were over. We had plans that would never come to fruition, and they played out behind my closed, crying eyes for days, a tapestry of my confirmed failure. Our parting was no surprise to me, but our friends and family were shocked, and a few even seemed personally hurt by our decision. After Facebook told our current and former classmates we'd ended things, a girl I'd known since middle school stopped in her tracks upon seeing me and wailed, "Ashley! What happened?! Not you and Brett!"

The breakup came right before college finals, and though I was sick in my sadness, I made it to every single class and ended the semester with my best grades yet. Now I was just waiting to go home, sit on the couch with my grandmother, work four different jobs, and try to make the best of what was beginning to look like a life that had lost its potential. I had been following my boyfriend's lead for six years because I didn't want to lead myself, and now I was alone.

To make matters worse, Brett was my co-worker at one of my jobs. Before we broke up, we'd both signed on to help our former marching band director with the incoming band members. Yes, I worked with my now ex-boyfriend at eight o'clock in the morning, five days a week, for an entire summer. We were cordial, and even hung out outside of work a few times, though less so as it became increasingly awkward. Brett really wanted to be friends, and I really didn't want to be by myself.

The night Brett came to my dorm room, the night he told me he was gay, there was a moment when I tried to leave. My clothes started to feel tight, and I felt like my circulation was being cut off, and I wanted to run into the hallway for air, but Brett fell to the floor, grabbed my leg, and said, "Please don't go." He had been holding on to me for six years. He liked me. I was his best friend. He was trying so hard to love me, and had been for so long. The sex was a goodbye—and, incidentally, the best we'd ever had. There is something different about the way the body moves when people tell each other the truth. This was my first real heartbreak, and it only hurt so bad because while he left me, he begged me not go.

One evening, after leaving one of my four jobs for the day and using my iron will to not call or text Brett, I decided to spend a little time with my grandmother. We sat across from each other on twin couches while I curled up with a fresh bag of chocolate chip cookies and hit play on *Diary of a Mad Black Woman* for the two millionth time (at least) that summer. My grandmother enjoyed this film, but after a few viewings she was a little less than enthused to be watching it once again. She pinned me from the corner of her eye.

"Girl, you must be hurting real bad," she said. I ignored the comment.

Two weeks earlier, she had said to me, "I hate that you and Brett broke up. You know, you'll probably never find anybody that'll treat you that well again." I had long ago learned that tact was not her strong suit, and so I tended to avoid, as much as humanly and respectfully possible, talking to her about my romantic life. With a mouthful of chocolate chip goodness and eyes set on the television screen, I gave a quick nod, already dreading the lecture that was surely to follow. My grandmother loved to tell people about themselves, and I might have been her favorite person to get together.

"You know, you shouldn't let yourself be bitter," she said.

"I'm not bitter, Grandma," I said. "Brett and I are still friends."

"You are bitter. You're mad at him. You're mad at yourself. You want to punish everybody, but you're too nice for that, so the only person you're punishing is you. That's why you eat cookies that don't make you feel good, you don't try to do anything with yourself before you leave the house, and you watch these sad-ass movies all the time."

"I'm not bitter, Grandma."

"Whatever. Just know that being bitter is swallowing poison and expecting the other person to die. You're not killing your body, but you are killing your spirit."

I stayed quiet and kept watching the movie, trying to seem unaffected by her words, and probably failing. I didn't want to be mad at Brett or scared of myself, and I didn't want to keep watching this movie over and over until I died. I didn't want to be bitter. I didn't want my grandmother to be right, and I didn't want to prove her right. And then I asked myself a question I hadn't asked myself in a long time: *What do you want?*

I'd stopped being a theater kid so that I could be more practical. I'd changed my college major four times already. I'd had countless jobs, taken a range of classes, and overworked myself trying to get closer to everything I *wanted*, and I didn't know what that was. I'd been expecting Brett to tell me or show me. I hadn't trusted myself to know what I wanted, and now I was afraid I'd forgotten how.

Four days later, I quit the job I was working with Brett two weeks early and went back to school. I decided to spend what was left of my summer finding out what made me happy. I took long walks in my favorite park, browsed used bookstores for paperbacks I'd loved as a kid, and listened to my favorite music turned up as loud as I wanted whenever I got into my car.

One day I used a new camera to begin taking nude portraits of myself. In those photos, I found a beauty I hadn't known lived right here, in me, and on this skin. I'd only been made to feel beautiful by a look or a compliment from Brett, maybe even having my face caressed by the same hand that played music in a way that made it zip from the top to the bottom of my spine. But now, seeing a photo of myself, my eyes staring back at me, I saw beauty. I whispered to myself, "It's you, girl. It's all you."

I was still me. No part of me had walked away with Brett, and there was no reason to blame or punish myself for being on my own. More importantly, I didn't want to do that to myself. I'd felt split apart inside, but all the pieces were here, within me. In the end, when I thought I'd run out of places to look, I found my broken heart had been sewn together by own hand. My hand, alone. I belonged to and was led by no one but myself. Finally, I began to trust myself to be on my own side.

THE FREEDOM OF ME

TANYA BLOUNT-TROTTER

THE MOMENT I KNEW THAT MY PARENTS WOULD never live under the same roof again, I began living on the path of fear. I didn't know it then, but this was the first of four major life events that would eventually help me realize that the only one holding me back in my life was myself.

I was eight years old when my parents got divorced. The image of my mom telling my dad to leave after his many affairs replayed in my head for years. I vividly remember my brother, sister, and me standing at the front door as my parents said their goodbyes. I was devastated, overwhelmed by a sense of loss and fear.

My dad was the apple of my eye. I could see no wrong in him. He was funny and light-spirited, and despite what was happening between my parents, I knew he loved me and my siblings. His absence and my mother's depression created anxiety in me. It seemed as though when my father left, the happiness in my mother disappeared too, and then even the happiness in myself. It was as if a part of me had died. It wasn't a physical death, but this unwanted change sure felt like it.

It didn't help that my mom didn't want anyone to know what was going on inside of our home. She was a very private woman who proudly handled things on her own. We couldn't talk about the divorce, and that was that. In the aftermath, my mother went into serious survival mode. She handled everything. She had no family or friends, and she had to create a life for her three young children. She was from another country (Panama) and in a place that was unfamiliar. The one thing she couldn't take care of was the feelings inside me—the fear and anxiety that overtook me when my father left. As I look back, I know now that it wasn't that she wouldn't, it was simply that she couldn't. She had her own pain to deal with.

Here I was, an eight-year-old girl, crazy about her dad who was now gone. What would I do with that emotion? Who could I talk to? My parents' divorce was the beginning of my feelings of powerlessness, being unheard and devalued. I felt stuck, and in return I became angry. I allowed this anger to dominate me because I didn't know any other way.

The second life-changing event was being pregnant with my son in my late thirties. My pregnancy brought up so many emotions. Pregnancy made me feel out of control. The hormones, the changes to my body, the fears that ran through my mind, and the health of my unborn child were constant reminders that I was not in control. Those fears had me overeating, working out way too much in my second trimester, and calling my doctor for any little thing that felt wrong. I was simply a drama queen.

I listened to all of the crazy stories about having a child in your thirties. I read all of the negative comments in pregnancy chat rooms about putting your kid in school. Fear dominated me in what was supposed to be one of my life's most amazing experiences. I was petrified. I was having a child at an older age than I'd expected, and I allowed my fear to rule my life and pregnancy.

The third event that turned my life upside down was the unexpected death of my mother. It made me feel completely out of control. Anyone who knows me knows I don't like surprises. Actually, I hate surprises. Surprises make me feel out of control. I always need to know what is going on and why. But death didn't care about any of my idiosyncrasies. Death came with a vengeance. No apologies and no preparation. It was in control and it came to teach me about myself.

The final event had to do with my marriage to my

husband, Michael. When we got married, I didn't know that after serving in the U.S. Army and going to war, he was suffering from combat PTSD. Finding all of this out three years into our marriage made me very, very angry. I was angry at myself for not knowing how to respond and for not having the knowledge I needed to support him the best that I could, and furious at the lack of help offered to him by the federal system. As a kid I was angry at my parents for getting a divorce but didn't know how to say it. Now, as an adult, I was once again overwhelmed with intense anger I was not prepared to process, involving another man I loved.

These were the four events that shaped me, and how I viewed them almost ruined the life I was meant to live.

My parents' divorce left me in fear, a fear the birth of my son heightened. The death of my mother left me feeling out of control. Finally, finding out that my marriage had an unwanted visitor called PTSD made me feel angry and powerless. This vicious cycle kept appearing in my life—fear, feeling out of control, and anger.

After my parents' divorce, living with the anxiety of "what if?" was the norm for me. Then, having my son in my late thirties made me further descend into a world of terrifying what-ifs. That negativity always loomed over me. What if this relationship doesn't work out? What if my son doesn't make it? What if I'm not successful? These thoughts controlled me, and I completely bought into the saying "Plan for the best but expect the worst." That became my mantra.

Ruled by fear and anger, I was always judging, always comparing, always feeling like I had to dim my light to allow someone else's to shine. I was skilled at seeing the beauty that lies inside of others, skilled at giving space to others to express how they felt, but too afraid to see the beauty inside of me. I was not fair to myself. I was too afraid to ask to be seen. I was too afraid to confront my own beauty because, to the person inside of me, not feeling seen or heard felt normal.

The burden of carrying around fear, depression, negative thoughts, loss of control and power, and guilt coupled with the inability to share these feelings left me completely exhausted. I grew tired of the drama controlling every thought in my head. I so desperately wanted to change the narrative I had created about myself and my life. As the great Maya Angelou said, "Every storm runs out of rain." I wanted to believe one day the storm would run out for me, too.

My path toward freedom began one sunny Friday in Maryland in 2010, before the last three major events in my life had happened. A tumultuous relationship had landed me back living in my mother's house. I was at rock bottom with no coping skills to deal with my pain, and decided to start seeing a therapist. I had no car and even had to borrow money from my parents to pay for therapy. I remember sitting in her office while she looked at my paperwork and hearing her say, "Why are you so angry?" She was not trying to fix me. She wasn't trying to change who I was or take away my feelings—she was just trying to help me explore who I was and what was going on with me. It was the first time in my life I felt like someone was listening, like someone actually saw me.

Week after week she would ask questions, and after a while, I started to see how the pain of my parents' divorce negatively controlled every decision I made. I started to wonder if I might be able to value my own opinion. I started to reconnect with the positive voice inside of me that had been hidden for so many years. I wanted to partner with that voice for the rest of my life. I no longer wanted to hide my uniqueness. My confidence grew, and I started to feel secure in my own greatness. But three of my major life events were still in my future, and my brand-new beliefs about myself and my place in the world would be put to the test.

Ten years later, my mother passed. After the pain, shock, and loneliness started to melt away, I began to remember what I had learned in therapy to help deal with my grief. People were telling me the pain would subside and I had to get on with my life because that's what my mom would have wanted. I found myself getting angry and, once again, feeling unheard and devalued. But then I remembered how my therapist had taught me to be curious about my feelings, not ignore them. When I was eight, I had felt I needed to hide my feelings about my parents and their divorce. But now I was no longer a child. I was a woman with her own thoughts. I had a voice. I mattered. After three weeks of trying to shove down my emotions rather than processing them, I decided to surround myself with people who would listen and understand. It was okay for me to not be okay. Unlike with the divorce of my parents, it was okay for me to come undone and share how I felt with others.

I continued to try to apply this new narrative to challenges as they came. I found peace with the PTSD in my marriage once I realized that while our marriage might be affected by episodes and occasional blow-ups, those things didn't have to *define* the marriage. I couldn't control my husband's PTSD, but I could control how it impacted us. I knew I wasn't powerless because I had the power of love guiding me.

Most of my life I believed everything that was holding me back was external. I convinced myself the reason I wasn't moving forward was because of the people affecting my life. "Look at what they did to me" used to be the excuse I used when any situation didn't work out in my favor. "Opportunities never come my way" is what I told myself. *Other* people were the reason why nothing in my home, career, or anywhere else was working.

After these four major life events—and realizing that I had not only survived them but gotten through them with a broader, truer understanding of myself—I started to see the world with different eyes. I apologized to myself for accepting these mental and emotional constraints for three decades. I began to practice self-care and acceptance. I allowed myself the grace to make mistakes. I had to learn how to be free again. Free like I was before that devastating day on the front steps of our home when my parents decided their marriage was over. I came to the realization that in times where I feel vulnerable or weak, I am beautiful and my experiences, even though they can be painful, also offer beauty.

Experiencing the pain of PTSD with my family made me vulnerable. And in that vulnerability, I found strength. I could show other wives and husbands and mothers and fathers how to care for their loved ones who were suffering. I could show them a marriage that had been tested by the disease yet still thrives. My experience mattered, and I could use it to help others.

The death of my mother taught me that everything I had ever learned about death was wrong, including how I grieved. My grief did not need to be rushed. And the fragility of my grief was rooted in unconditional love. On the day that she died, my father waited in the car until she took her last breath before coming into the hospital room with tears in his eyes. It made me realize that despite my misconceptions about their relationship, they had already made their peace, and in turn, that helped me find mine. We are all just passing through this journey called life, and we had better live and love like there's no tomorrow because there may never be a tomorrow.

Death taught me to make my existence count and, more importantly, to find a reason for it to count. There is a legacy greater than any material object or idea, and that legacy is love. It transcends money, success, and power. Like the air we breathe, we all need it and we all know that we cannot survive without it.

Greatness does not lie in depression, fear, uncertainty, and pain. I've had to face those things when they weighed me down. I've had to own up to my part in it all even if it wasn't my fault. When I was old enough to know that I needed help, it was up to me to get the help. No one was going to do it for me. My greatness lies inside of me. Through these four experiences, I have learned that when I am standing inside of my own greatness, I shine a light on everyone around me: my husband, my children, my family, my friends, and everyone involved in my career. Everyone reaps the benefits of me being who I am.

The most courageous thing I have ever done is change the way I thought about myself and the major events in my life that helped shape me. It took me a while to get there, but eventually I did. I had to think differently about myself and circumstances, and with that understanding came freedom. Freedom is a birthright, and I am grateful that I'm no longer enslaved by a life of mediocrity. I am no longer a burden to myself. I am free to be me.

PERIOD PLAYLIST

AMENA BROWN

MY MOM HAD THREE BASIC RULES WHEN WE LEFT HER house to go anywhere: "Don't touch nothing. Don't break nothing. Do not embarrass me." She'd usually say this through gritted teeth, then smile at whoever passed us in the store or whoever greeted us at someone else's home. I would stick my arms to my sides as if they were glued there while we walked through the store, or sit as if my hands were stapled to my lap at the home of my mom's friends, beginning to believe that embarrassment was a spill that could never be cleaned up.

The first time my mom explained the biology of my period, I was nine years old, staring at the green tile of my grandmother's bathroom. With my mom's knowledge as a nurse, she took a scientific approach, describing to me the journey of red and white blood cells and what would happen to them when they shed. She told me what sounded like the science fiction story of a uterus caterpillar who shed her skin, bled, became a butterfly, and planned to transform me into a woman. Every month. It sounded dangerous, weird, painful, and like nothing I should look forward to.

When I started my period at age fourteen, it was clear having a period was like so many things I was implicitly told about being a woman: be quiet, be strong, keep up appearances. I had been taught to hide my period, to not talk about my period, to do my best to act like I wasn't on my period, to pretend away any pain caused by my period. I had been taught to equate my period with shame—shame for being a woman, for having feelings, for feeling even the slightest bit of anger or frustration. I had been taught to see my period as an embarrassment, as a nuisance, as a negative thing.

So I decided to start giving my period the talk.

Don't touch nothing.

Don't break nothing.

Do not embarrass me.

But apparently, periods are not good listeners. At some point in my monthly life there will be cramps, headaches, backaches, moodiness, and fatigue. There will be blood. There will be trips to the bathroom that feel like a crime scene. There will be decisions about tampons or pads or cups, about light, thin, wings, super-absorbent, overnight. I will see these categories and wonder if I am preparing for my period or packing luggage for a trip on a plane and deciding which bags to check.

There will be the times my period decides to surprise me and there are no tampons, pads, cups, wings, carry-ons, personal bags, panty liners, or ocean liners, and I will have to become a quick inventor, a period MacGyver, fashioning a period product out of three paper towels, six squares of bathroom tissue, two Band-Aids, and a prayer. There will be the outfits ruined by my period, the resuscitation I tried on my favorite pants hoping they would survive the bloodstain. How I stood pantsless in a hotel bathroom and transformed into a scientist, Googling the concoction that could remove blood from houndstooth pants, finding out that I must blot, pat, apply cold water, and rub together, but not sure if I should do this to the pants or my thighs or both. Many of my favorite pairs of underwear have been lost as casualties: even after being scrubbed to oblivion, they could not be saved or rescued and instead had to be mourned and then thrown away.

My period requires a certain type of underwear artillery: the granny panty, the full coverage, the time-of-the-month drawers, the kind of underwear that nearly comes up to my belly button and covers my whole backside, rumpus, ba-donk-a-donk-donk. Thank you, Missy Elliott. This means all other types of underwear, including parachutes, zip lines, cheekies, and G-strings, are reserved for the rest of the month.

I have learned not to waste cute, fashionable panties on my period. During that week, my vagina has other things to be concerned about and lace sliding into my crevasses is not one of them.

I have panicked in a bathroom at someone else's home about the lack of bathroom tissue and an empty open trash can, wondering how I am supposed to make my discarded period products look like normal trash. I have wrapped them up in bathroom tissue until they are mummified enough to possibly be confused for a random time someone else needed to practice the art of origami with bathroom tissue only to throw it away.

People with periods are maligned and marginalized for being too emotional, too hormonal, too affected by the sway of our cycles, when in actuality we continue to work in politics, run companies, boss up, parent, breathe, make art, make decisions, show up to work, and show up for our families and friends, all while managing minor to major pain and discomfort every month or so. Then when we speak up for ourselves, assert our thoughts and opinions, say no, or boldly raise our voices, we are suspected and proven guilty of being a bitch and probably being on our periods.

My friends and I talked openly about our periods, the symptoms we experienced, the period mishaps we knew all too well. Some of my girlfriends who had become mothers shared how they were approaching the period talk with their daughters. They told us how they were encouraging their daughters to remember that help for a period mishap was as close as the woman next to you.

I thought about all the times I'd dished about period cramps with a woman I was meeting for the first time, or the times I'd reached into some forgotten nook in my purse to retrieve a period product I'd forgotten I had so I could help a woman I'd just met in a public bathroom. Having a period means being a part of a community where we are not alone, where our periods can transform from a place of embarrassment to a place of empowerment.

My period didn't deserve the talk I'd been giving it. Everything I said or thought about my period affected the way I spoke or thought about myself. I needed to develop a new talk for myself. As a woman. As a Black woman. As an artist. I needed to set different expectations for myself and my body.

So I decided to stop being mean to my period and to myself. My period is not a place for shame. My period isn't a nuisance. I discovered that maybe my period is actually a place to be reminded that I am empowered. My period is a motivational speaker with a story to tell.

So I did what I usually do when I want to feel motivated: I made a playlist for my period.

I received my first mixtape when I was in high school. My friend had commandeered a blank tape that belonged to his parents, painted Wite-Out over the label, and wrote on top of it "The Fugees, The Score." I didn't know I'd fall in love with the power a repurposed cassette tape could have. How it could tell someone you loved them or how much you loved a new band or how excited you were to have a new friend. I recorded songs off of the radio, trying my best to press stop before the deejay started to talk. My friends and I passed cassettes between us like notes during class.

By the time I went to college, cassettes had been replaced by CDs. I learned my computer had the power to burn a CD of songs I loved, so I made mix CDs. My younger sister introduced me to Lupe Fiasco on a purple CD she burned for me. I made mix CDs for my car and as birthday gifts. I made mix CDs of love songs even when I was afraid to tell the object of my affection I was falling in love with them.

When my husband and I first started dating, I created my last mix CD. I could no longer hide my deep and giddy feelings for him when I not only made him a mix CD of songs that reminded me of him but took the time to type explanations for each one. Eventually CDs were replaced by iPods and MP3 players, and those were replaced by smartphones. I discovered I could show my mixtape love through making playlists.

I make playlists for everything that's important to me: for when I feel insecure, for when I want to celebrate, for when I'm getting ready for a show, for when I work out, for when I need to muster up all of my woman confidence. So yes, my period deserved a playlist too.

My period playlist begins with rapper Bone Crusher's hit "Never Scared." Accompanied by a rumbling synthesizer and a banging drum kit, Bone Crusher pontificates about how someone outside of the club has mistaken him for someone who should be messed with. How he has certain "tools" in his trunk that can be used to assuage any doubts harbored by this passerby.

My period brain is a Bone Crusher concert, my eye twitching at the thought that anyone might test me, question me, or any way disrespect me. I am yelling "I AIN'T NEVER SCARED" everywhere I go, from the grocery store to the bank, in a work meeting and at a family gathering.

Bone Crusher probably has no idea that he not only created the perfect period theme song but also crafted an accurate music video to go with it. In this video, Bone Crusher becomes a giant, traipsing through Atlanta's highways and byways, causing Godzilla-sized trouble while shouting the names of the various sides of town he is apparently unafraid of. It appears he even takes the time to play hopscotch on one of the city's busy streets, causing mayhem and not apologizing for it. The curls from his Afro are moving to their own beat as he and his squad yell "never scared" while giant Bone Crusher crushes cars and buildings with his sneakers like so many Tic Tacs underfoot. ATTEN-CHUN.

Rapper Killer Mike, who is featured on the song, describes his weapon of choice in said "never scared" situations as a gun that has permanent PMS. Maybe they did know they were making a period theme song?

As Bone Crusher's hands decide the best thing for them to do is randomly grab at a whole story of windows on a skyscraper, I ponder my own period-motivated actions. Bone Crusher, I too have what feels like a Heavy Chevy pounding through my abdomen.

Next on my period playlist is LL Cool J's "Mama Said Knock You Out." I hear Sly and the Family Stone singing and I hear LL Cool J rapping lines that my period knows all too well. LL Cool J is ready for a fight and my period is too. My period knows what it's like to call it a comeback. My period has been here for years. I am also crying tears like a monsoon. If my period's name is Mama, she intends to knock anyone and everyone out in the process, including me.

LL Cool J begins this video with a hoodie over his head in the corner of a boxing ring. Why yes, LL, how did you know this is exactly how my period starts? Yes, LL, I too have wanted to knock someone out. I too have wished for a microphone to drop down from the ceiling toward the random boxing ring in which I find myself so that I can yell all manner of threats and obscenities to anyone who would dare try me. And when LL yells "damage" and "destruction," I have never felt more seen.

When I have period rage, I listen to Beyoncé's "Don't Hurt Yourself" and Cardi B's "Bodak Yellow." When I need a good period cry, I listen to Kelly Clarkson's "Breakaway" and Alanis Morissette's "Ironic." Sometimes my period is a heavy metal rager, sometimes it's a raucous hip-hop show, and sometimes it is a Lilith Fair mess of feelings. My period playlist is full of songs that help me celebrate my rage and affirm the badassness of my womanhood.

When I listen to these songs, I remember periods are complicated. Some of us never get a period. Some of us have feared the months our period arrived late or didn't arrive at all. Some of us can't afford or don't have access to period products. Some of us have longed for the moment our period's tardy arrival would produce a positive pregnancy test, but each month our period arrives on time. Some of our periods bring us an immeasurable amount of pain. Some of our periods remind us that our biology is betraying our gender identity.

As I learn to accept my period, I'm learning to accept myself. As I am. Complications and all.

Now I know: my period is fearless. She arrives without being concerned about what anyone thinks of her. She takes up her space with no apology. She decides to be heavy or light based on her own whims, not to impress anyone.

She's nosy. She asserts herself in my personal life, speaking truth to me like a good friend should. She convinces me that sleep is the best use of my time. She yells at me that I deserve better! She hypes me up until I demand fair pay, assume that every donut is my soul mate, and stop wasting time on things and people that drain me. My period is a truth detector, a special kind of polygraph. She pushes me to be honest when I don't like something, to speak up when I'm irritated, to leave when I'm no longer having a good time—at a party, in an outfit, or in a relationship.

Each time my period shows up, she reminds me to be gentle, honest, bold, and brave—to honor her as I honor myself. Because my period is me. She says the things I really think. She reminds me to be my full self always. And that is a rhythm worth listening to.

ON THE HORRORS OF FITTING IN

CAMERON ESPOSITO

I WAS OUT WALKING THE SILVER LAKE RESERVOIR, A blacktop-rimmed body of water on the east side of Los Angeles known for its jogging paths and celebrity sightings, in my usual fashion—alone, earbudded, and playing one song on repeat—when I ran into my long-time friend Emily. We hadn't connected in years, but she paused her run to ask how I was doing, and I said, "I'm trying to get into running. Can I run with you sometime?" Before that popped out of my mouth, I hadn't for one second been trying to get into running. I was, however, ten months into the separation that would eventually become a divorce, and had reached the zenith of my lifelong need to be apart. For maybe the first time in my adult life, I was ready to engage.

Emily and I met in Chicago. We didn't do exactly

the same thing—I'm a stand-up comic and she worked in the adjacent world of musical improv. Emily occasionally did stand-up too, but it wasn't make-or-break for her the way it was for me. She had other things to pin her future on—like work at the famed Second City theater or with her own musical improv touring company.

I had done improv during and after college, but by the time I met Emily, I had no interest in group warm-ups, audience-less rehearsals, or post-show drunken recaps of our best collective moments. I felt so much shame—from a childhood of not quite fitting with gender norms and time I spent closeted at Catholic school—and the only way I could function was by screaming (well, eloquently speaking) my truth uninterrupted, mic in hand. Improv is all teamwork and creating agreed-upon, cooperative art. I wanted none of that. My whole being ached to break free in soliloquy. So I switched to stand-up, and there found space to speak. What I lost was a space to belong.

Each night, before going up onstage, I warmed up as all comics do: by lurking in the back of the room, silently judging everyone else's jokes, and furiously scribbling my notes on a bar napkin or in a falling-apart notebook that barely held together a massive series of similarly scrawled set lists. It looked like the work of a psychopath—like evidence of mania left at a crime scene—and I loved that about the job, that it required such singular, adrenaline-fueled focus and so much interior exploration.

Because stand-up is all interior. A comic's aloof pronouncements may be delivered so engagingly that it seems like the comic is actually part of what's going on in the room, in culture, in our own lives. But we aren't. Comics comment. We don't engage, even when we get engaged, which is a pun because I married another comic. To me, my spouse and I felt apart from the world, untouchable, removed, and therefore at the center of it all. It was my job to discuss all news, have a take on every show, each event, everything in my own life and all parts of culture, and I brought that home with me. We *discussed*.

When I found stand-up I thought it was a cure for shame. I thought I would outsmart other people's laughter, set myself apart from judgment by making myself the judge. Years ago, after I already felt I'd made it in stand-up, I had the unsettling realization that I would never be able to attend my own shows. I'd *be* the show, sure, but I'd never be *at* one. The groups of queer friends laughing their heads off, the dates that looked like they were going well and those that appeared to be flopping—I'd never be part of any of it. I'd created for others the safety I needed myself.

My trade doesn't breed a strong co-worker mentality. We start out competing with one another for the best jokes at open mics, but at that level, there's a social element to stand-up. At least there seemed to be for the straight dude comics around me. I always felt a bit like someone's younger sister who's been trying to break into the boys-only clubhouse. Later, when I started doing well enough to headline shows, travel, create work for TV, etc., even that vague camaraderie was lost. Everyone else was out headlining their own shows, too. I started my career looking for space, and as success, or at least survival, came into focus, the adrenaline faded, the challenge dulled, the need to express my deepest pain mellowed. All I was left with was space.

And I still love my job, but it is not a cure for shame. Experienced without balance, stand-up is a crutch. It addresses shame by placing the hurt little kid inside every comic (you non-comics have a hurt little inner kid, too) in a cooler-than-thou wrapping. At one point, that wrapping saved my life. Over time, it became an albatross. Cool guys can rarely relax.

To deal with the anxiety brought on by staying so apart, so outwardly unaffected, I spent large chunks of each day out walking. New to a city where I didn't know anyone, with a full weekend of shows ahead and a job that starts at 8 P.M., I'd walk my days away, occasionally visiting the shoe repair place in my neighborhood after returning home to have my soles replaced before continuing to lope along blocks and blocks of Los Angeles solo. I had tons of acquaintances, but there wasn't really anyone I knew in my town, either.

So when Emily texted me to follow up on our conversation, I suggested a time and place to meet the following day and set my trail-dusty not-running sneakers next to my bed for early morning ease. The first time we ran together, I made it about fifty steps before having to walk. Previously, this is the sort of moment that would have made me want to leave town, move home to my parents' basement, and never be seen in these parts again. It is my preference to appear composed, masterful, fucking good at the thing I'm doing, and instead here I was, red-faced and panting. Still, I stayed. In fact, we made a plan to meet up at the same time the following week.

Despite my slowing her down, Emily stayed with me. We didn't talk. We ran. We walked. We ran some more. I let her see my heaving-chest-bad-at-this crumbling mess of a self not just that one day, but for weeks. Each week we met and I asked to stop and gasped and made it just a few steps farther. Months later, I made it the full two miles around the reservoir. Even by then I wasn't fast or fluid or gazelle-like, and two miles wasn't the marathon I'd set my mind to running after our first conversation, but it was a goal slowly achieved *with* someone.

I wasn't new to being an athlete. In a feat of white

suburbanism, I played on about eight million sports teams growing up, everything from golf to tennis to soccer, basketball, volleyball, and softball, and I swam. After swim practice, I'd shower off, toss on a jersey, and ride my bike to a softball game, each day a sort of triathlon, which worked for me. I've always loved a goal, and the directness of sports made sense to me. Even if I wasn't terribly talented, the games and seasons were finite. I never had any illusion about playing in the WNBA or swimming in the Olympics. I was good enough to get through tryouts, good enough to blend in—playing on a team meant that I was fitting in. That I was good enough, period.

And I took ballet for eight years of my childhood—from ages two to ten—and with that came goals never achieved. The impossible-to-wriggle-into pink tights. The swimsuit-outside-the-water leotards. The lean femininity and emphasis on grace. The hyperattention paid to each detail of my tiny kid body. Maybe this is where my wanting to leave the group began—I felt body-patrolled, gender-patrolled, outside the norm, and never enough. Rather than continue to stick it out in dance class, I opted instead to leave altogether.

My sister, Allyson, took dance, too. She was three years older, hated team sports, and seemed to fit with the older girls in her class as they all chattered in the locker room. She stuck with dancing—still dances, actually—and later added yoga and CrossFit; she's fluent in basically any fitness experience where one might wear a racerback top and, generally, Lycra.

When we lived in the same city, Allyson routinely invited me along to the classes she'd take. The collective feeling of team sports didn't transfer to the adult version of fitness—I didn't want to be noticed trying to do something I wasn't good at. It's one thing to be an energetic, gung-ho little kid playing with a team and have your effort noticed. By my adulthood, I felt I was supposed to be good at everything I tried.

So I always declined, except for a brief stretch when I felt brave enough to try a popular yoga studio my sister recommended because it was known for this one very calm, inclusive queer teacher. I then dated and broke up with that calm, inclusive queer teacher, which made classes there a lot less calm, and I stopped going. From then on, few things brought greater horror into my heart than the idea of group fitness, which has no season but an emphasis on constant self-improvement and maintenance. More comfortable commenting on culture than joining the tide, I preferred to not compete with the ever-fit. In fact, my list of biggest horrors goes: systemic societal injustice, bugs that fly, group fitness.

Which is why, when I had the urge to text my friend Tatiana a few months ago, it indicated a massive shift on my part. It was 9 P.M. on a Saturday night and I was pondering her weekly habit of attending a ninety-minute hip-hop aerobics dance class every Sunday at 10 A.M. because I thought maybe, just maybe, I'd meet her there. I didn't *want* to meet her there; I was experiencing a post-divorce willingness to try new things brought on by sadness that had become too big and isolation that had become too extreme. I didn't feel an influx of confidence so much as a push of desperation. I was desperate enough to do the nearly impossible thing that is asking to be included. My running with Emily had been a baby step, but now I wanted to take a bigger one and go to an actual g-d aerobics class.

"Are you going tomorrow?" I hit send and stared at my phone. I hoped Tatiana would never respond. Or that she'd respond, "Absolutely not. The studio where it's held fell directly into the center of the earth. No one was hurt. The earth just opened and pulled it in." And that I, in turn, would get to think, "Wow. I was willing to try something I might be bad at, but was prevented from doing so by an act of the cosmos. I guess I will stick with things I know I am good at, like stand-up comedy and walking long distances while listening to an audiobook and avoiding eye contact with strangers." Imagine my disappointment when Tatiana's name flashed on my screen alongside a warm, all-caps "YEP! Wanna meet me there?" It wasn't the first time she'd asked me to attend with her, but it was the first time when I thought: fuck it. "Yes," I typed, before throwing my phone across the room but onto a pillow because I don't have phone-smashing money.

And so, thirty-eight years old, having not been to a dance class in more than twenty-five years, I woke up to my alarm, threw on some basketball shorts that I hoped would work for class, and went to meet Tatiana. I stretched, I moved around, I sweated my ass off. I went that week and every Sunday for the following month. I told my friend Kelli I'd been going and she asked to come along, loved it, and invited me to the queer and body-positive aerobics class she attends, which I, in turn, went to as well. And from there I got invited to a roller-skating party and a series of barre classes and a beginner ballet intensive and an afternoon clubbing session in a darkened warehouse space that sounds way more *Euphoria* than it was. I said yes to all of it.

And finally I felt some relief. I'm not a trained dancer, I fell roller-skating, and I may never run a marathon. I am not always cool and not everything in my life is easy or taken at a distance. I cry every time the flag is presented at a sporting event. I love following the rules and I love Céline Dion. And despite my continued preference for stand-up over improv, I play well with others. I am more than an observer, and I gave up dancing like no one was watching because I prefer making direct eye contact with my friends and smiling my head off during dance class.

The fear that the people around me will notice me, will see me participating and shame me for it—I am throwing that away. I'm no longer choosing to position myself outside of life. And sure, most evenings I am still the show. But on weekends and in the mornings, I'm one of the crowd, part of the group, finding space without isolation. And it feels good.

THE VIEW

MICHAEL TROTTER JR.

RECENTLY I HAVEN'T BEEN FEELING SEXY AT ALL. I used to think it was because I was overweight, but I know some sexy people who are considered borderline obese. When I look in the mirror, I see what I could be. I see little signs of muscle here and there. But when I leave the mirror, that's really where my issues begin. I remember watching professional wrestling as a teen and seeing bodies like The Rock's or Triple H's, or looking at movies and seeing Vin Diesel or Morris Chestnut and thinking to myself, *If I had their bodies, would that make me sexy?* I would judge my SEXINESS by the attention I would get from the opposite sex, whether it was my wife or some random look of interest from a stranger. YES! IT FEELS GOOD TO BE

WANTED. But it feels even better to be wanted by the one you love.

My relationship with my body hit an all-time low one particular day in 2015. I had been feeling like a king all day not because of how I looked, but because I was knee-deep in purpose. Earlier that day, I had been a guest speaker at a motivational event for veterans. In the afternoon, I had officiated at the funeral service of a very special lady whose life had been claimed by gun violence, and through my speech I was able to get twenty young people to commit to a life of love over hate. Now I was off to see my beautiful baby receive the Mission of Love Decatur "Bucky" Trotter Humanitarian Award for her efforts with her organization, I Am Beautiful Corporation. All was well. Except for one thing: I had no clue what I was going to wear. I had recently lost a good deal of weight and donated all of my clothes to charity because they didn't fit. I owned three pairs of jeans, one pair of dress slacks, two white dress shirts, one brown dress shirt, and one pair of gray Dockers that were inappropriate to wear to this kind of event. But the universe provides, and my friend James came downstairs with seven dress shirts that were all pressed, some still with the tag on them. Now I was ready to go to the ball.

At the event, James took a snapshot of Tanya and me seated and hugging each other. I was so eager to see the picture because I knew we looked good, but when I looked at the photo, all I saw was the weight I hadn't lost yet.

I should have been enjoying the event, but instead my head filled with negative thoughts about how I looked. Why was my belly taking its time and not falling in line? Should I not eat tonight, tomorrow, or the next day? Maybe I should go on a fast? Yeah, that'll do it. After considering all these ridiculous options, I finally heard the voice of truth: "HEY, MAN, GET A GRIP! It's just another point of view!" I realized that yes, I had come a long way, but there would likely always be some angles, some shots, some views of myself that I didn't care for. That's what "a work in progress" means.

See, we can't encourage ourselves by only embracing one point of view—the View. The View is what I see when I've trained myself to find what I'm looking for— like extra weight—rather than the joy and beauty in the picture.

Instead, we have to allow ourselves to embrace the FULL VIEW of ourselves. How can I say I see the big picture when I'm only looking through a little lens? Encouraging myself is not ignoring the FULL VIEW, but embracing the exciting work of changing THE VIEW.

From this experience, I learned that CHANGING THE VIEW and seeing the FULL VIEW of myself worked in four parts . . .

1. The OVERVIEW: My plan of attack, my goal.
2. The PREVIEW: What occurs when I am in motion toward revealing the future. It's how I'm going to look. If I look hard enough while working hard in the process, I will get little glimpses here and there that suggest I am on my way.
3. The VIEW: What I see when I am actually looking for a version of myself that I WOULD APPROVE OF.
4. The REVIEW: What I see when I have reached my goal. I review what took place in the process—for example, from the moment I gained excess weight to the moment I dropped it off.

In this process of becoming vulnerable with myself, I pondered the question "Why do I feel so unattractive and undesirable?" When I asked myself this question, I had to look at some of my personal characteristics. I wanted to get to the core of my feelings, period. Not just count it all toward being overweight. What I found was life-changing, and it is helping me even at this moment. Seeing myself as desirable, now that's a whole thing in itself! I am the kind of guy who loves attention. I love to make people laugh, and I love to help people out. I am all about being in love with someone special, but when you think about being in love with YOURSELF, most men don't know what that means. Most men measure their sexiness by SEX. But being sexy has nothing to do with sex. In fact, being sexy doesn't even lead to sex; INTIMACY leads to sex.

So, what leads to being SEXY? Here is what I have found to be true in my life. I feel SEXY when I am able to be myself. Like when I can help someone, or when I take a load off of my wife, I feel SEXY because I feel like I matter in this world. No one can make you feel SEXY. YOU make you feel SEXY. I initiate 90 percent of the intimate sexy moments with my wife; because she only initiates 10 percent, I could easily let that lower my level of feeling sexy and the tank would be near empty.

But I understand that I can't count on her to make me feel SEXY. I count on her to be intimate with me.

INTIMACY is not SEX, but it is companionship to the MAX. What I am learning is most men want more INTIMACY than women think. There are times when I simply want my wife to rub my feet while I rub hers or we sing to each other. I'd even take a healthy debate because it is engaging and I learn the depths of her intelligence. INTIMACY was never meant to be one moment in time. INTIMACY is a day-to-day, minute-to-minute, second-to-second workout that usually involves engaging with another person in transferring energy. But we come to that aha moment again where we learn that INTIMACY is also personal healing. So I have learned to be INTIMATE with myself. And I did this by changing THE VIEW I had of myself.

Today I am seeing MYSELF differently. I see my

weight as an INTIMATE space to personally heal what I have damaged. I see my character and attitude as a SEXY space where I can weed out the things that don't make me feel SEXY. I won't penalize others for the way they may try to make me feel, but I will walk the path of destiny and live my life as IMPACTFULLY as I can. I know that I cannot make another person feel SEXY, but I can give INTIMACY to the right people generating SEXY vibes within themselves.

EVERYONE in this world needs to feel SEXY! EVERYONE in this world needs to feel INTIMACY!

Coming from military life, I was taught not to feel. Don't feel pain, don't feel hurt, don't feel good. So you simply feel only disappointment, fear, and anxiety. I was numb. I was so numb that I never realized that I was going through life not paying attention to anything except myself. It was inevitable that I would miss moments that would define my current state.

My grandfather once told me that there are two moments in life that occur. One moment is considered the big moment because it is so enormous, so monumental, so massive that it cannot be contained. You know the cosmos orchestrated it because it is so glorious that you yourself are afraid of it. This moment is what I like to call "the pause" because it pauses whatever current state you're in and gives you a glimpse of your future, and you walk away from that moment both eager and attentive to your NOW!

The second moment is what I like to call "the breaking moment," the teaching moment in your history. It comes alongside "the pause"; however, it is not to be missed.

I am so thankful for lessons that break me. I've had moments in my life where I have walked around town with my head held too high, pompously flaunting my survival of the war, but not realizing my survival was possible only because of others' pain. During those moments, I needed more than a wake-up call. I needed a serious breaking. I needed to be humbled. I needed to be twisted and wrung out because not only was I hurting others, but I was filling myself with the soil of my own tears and it was making me bitter.

I discovered that I couldn't hide my emotions away forever because sooner rather than later, that version of myself before the pain, disappointment, and war wanted to come roaring forward, breaking through the face of the monster I was hiding behind.

I'm more than war. I'm more than a talent. I'm more than just Tanya's husband or Legend's daddy. I am Michael and yes, though I'm broken, I am breaking. Breaking down the barriers within me. I am breaking away from pain. I am breaking ties with hurt. I am breaking down the hardness and stony walls that rejection, resentment, and desertion told me I had to build to create safety. Those were lies, and I am now ready to live in my truth. I am love and I am breaking.

I didn't escape. I stopped running. I am now flat-footed, planted and grounded in this belief that I am meant to be free. Free from seeing myself through the dirty lenses of failure. I am free from seeing disappointment as my only deserving emotion. Yes, I am somebody special and unique. Born with a true purpose and a true calling to myself first. I am ready to love me and all of me for more than a second. I see my weight not as a distraction but instead as this wonderful and amazing opportunity to dig in and sculpt a work of art because of love and not pain. We have the power. We have the strength. We have the courage and the heart for this walk of life.

My mind is free from the negative stain of injustice I brought upon myself. Yes, I was once uncivil toward my peace. Yes, I was once uncompromising to my own liberty. Yes, I once ignored my right to the idea that I BELONG in the realm of togetherness. Yes, I was once convinced that I deserved only pain, and I would lie down to be walked all over. But now I have learned to cast down every stronghold, every negative remark, every guilty thought I bring upon myself. I see my bruises and I no longer cringe, but I smile because I understand I have conquered my new point of view. It wasn't easy. I bent and twisted until I broke wide open to release the bitterness I harbored inside for so long.

I broke. I changed my VIEW. I learned to LOVE MYSELF.

You can do this too. Know that you are part of a world with an army of overcomers. You are not alone. You see the mountain and now it's time to climb it. Take the fight and make it your own.

Whatever the "unflattering picture" might be in your life, remind yourself that you have the power to change your view and that it's never too late.

THAT TRAVELING HEAT

CONNIE LIM (MILCK)

FOR YEARS, I DIDN'T BELIEVE THAT PHYSICAL INTI-
macy was sacred. Instead, I operated as if I were on a
mission to convince myself that sex was a casual, flip-
pant thing, like a cheap pair of sunglasses that I might
look fashionable in, without risk of crying over them if
they broke or got misplaced: something delightful and
disposable.

I watched successful, beautiful, big-city women flip-
pantly refer to sex as a conquest on the edgy television
shows of the early 2000s. I found accomplices in the
male-dominated rooms I spent a lot of time in as a
budding singer-songwriter. My lips would curl into a
smug smile as I coolly cracked crude sex jokes around
my guy bandmates.

In college at UC Berkeley, I was known in the dorm halls as "Walking Sex." Yes, this is a true story, and that was actually my nickname. Insert face-palm emoji here. I didn't intentionally create this persona, but my desire to duck and dodge real intimacy somehow masked my inner nerdy, awkward tomboy who lived for reading a good self-help book. What people saw was a cool girl. I got good at pretending as if I were someone else, as if I were one of those fancy liberated women on TV.

Acting became my way of life, as I was deeply invested in protecting myself from a deeper pain. If I could walk, talk, joke, and laugh as if sex was no big deal, then maybe I could callous myself to the fact that I let my first boyfriend abusively manipulate me into having sex when I was not ready. Reframing something painful into something innocuous helped to numb the lingering sting.

The loss of my virginity to someone who forced me into it, the loss of trust in myself—I ran from this pain by putting on a front of calm and nonchalance. Yet underneath the surface, I blamed myself for allowing him to corner me into doing things I didn't want to do.

As much as I tried to run from my past, the memories persisted. I remember the first time he drunkenly threw his car keys at me. The keys whizzed just past the right side of my head, slamming against the wall behind me. He'd gotten upset that I pushed his hand away as he was trying to get into my jeans.

When I felt his rage fill the room, I decided that I needed to shrink. I needed to ignore that spell of heat that started in my belly and traveled up toward my neck, forming a bottleneck, a dense ball of weight that would render me silent. At age fourteen I didn't yet have the experience to know that that traveling heat was my personal alarm system. It was a signal sent by the deeper knowing guiding me, telling me to GET OUT.

Instead, I thought if I stayed quiet enough, I could disappear without disappearing. That if I could avoid getting in his way, I could prevent making him mad. For the next few months, I learned how to figuratively and literally bend and fold into awkward shapes so he could do as he pleased. I thought that if I could appease him, I could have some control over whether or not he'd hurt me.

Some of us run, some of us hide. Some of us fight back. This is when I learned that I am somebody who hides very well. Too well.

As I grew out of my teens and clawed my way out of that relationship, I got quite good at hiding in plain sight. I could map out my escape plans in any given situation while still keeping a calm, carefree smile on my face. "You're so calm and easy to be around, Connie!" people would say to me. Little did they know that my insides oftentimes felt like a frenzied chaos of quarantined people tugging at the exit doors of a badly lit hospital.

This dynamic of undercover anxiety continued for years. My insides were filled with voices telling me that I was bad, that something was inherently wrong with me to have attracted a guy like him. I couldn't let people know this secret about me, or they would leave me. So I played it all cool. I kept a distance from people in order to keep them close.

As years passed, I realized that my expertise in hiding had an unintended side effect: it rendered even myself clueless as to who I was. I was ill-equipped as an adult in the world, blinded by my eagerness to be anybody but myself. I had ignored the alarm systems and inner knowings so much that I didn't know how to listen for them. I found myself stumbling through adulthood, not knowing who I was. I was sick of being a stranger to myself and wanted to change.

Since my mind was filled with voices betraying me, I focused on the ancient wisdom of my body. I noticed that sometimes the traveling heat would flash through my legs and arms for about 1.5 seconds while I was having a conversation with a friend or co-writer. Other times I'd feel it when somebody would start talking shit about someone they claimed to care about. I

CONNIE LIM (MILCK)

started to listen more and more to that traveling heat. Now it's my guide; it's my body telling me to LISTEN CAREFULLY to what is happening in the moment, because there is something for me to learn or take note of.

I also realized that the traveling heat has led me not only away from danger but also toward my joy. For instance, as a young kid I would feel a restless heat ping-pong through my arms, hands, chest, and neck whenever I'd watch others singing onstage. I could barely sit still to watch music awards shows, as the idea of passively consuming would almost torture me. The traveling heat was doing its work on me. It was telling me that I didn't want to be entertained; I wanted to be the entertainer. The heat would continue nudging me into excitingly uncomfortable scenarios of performing my songs in front of friends and strangers. Open mics. Booking my own shows. Recording my own songs. Leaving my pre-med/pre-law/pre-business/pre-approved/daughter-of-Chinese-immigrants path.

After graduating from UC Berkeley, I listened to my body and moved to LA to pursue a career in music. As my passion for music and songwriting continued to blossom, I could feel my head hitting up against that good old glass ceiling. I was haunted by imposter syndrome.

I was still dragging around this narrative that I was

inherently bad or flawed; it was like a sack of boulders behind me. When music executives took meetings with me, I would shrink, fearing they'd see that I was, in fact, not worthy of the opportunity.

I couldn't build a healthy workflow with anybody in the business, because I was so afraid of someone hurling the metaphorical car keys at my head again. Instead of approaching people with my contentions or concerns, I would ghost them, or just hide in plain sight. When I would shrink like that, the quality of my music and relationships was compromised. When I was afraid to tell a producer I didn't like a sound that she chose, how was I supposed to manifest my vision?

My songs were my compass, and my fears were compromising their sense of direction. I started growing tired of watching myself getting in my own way, and I wanted to understand the root of my sabotage. And that is the moment that I bit the bullet and signed up for therapy.

"It's interesting how onstage, you have this big voice. Yet offstage, you have no voice." My therapist looked at me patiently as I sat there, stunned by her accurate perspective. The knife of truth cut me open, creating just enough of an opening for me to reclaim those lost parts of myself.

With the help of my therapist, I realized that what happened to me at age fourteen was not my fault. I had to repeat it over and over to myself, *Good Will Hunting* style: "It's not my fault. It's not my fault. It's not my fault." It took months for me to integrate this new idea. In fact, I sometimes still have to call my best friend to remind me that I didn't make it all up. The mind is very invested in protecting us from pain, and mine was trying to do so by fictionalizing my trauma.

Bravery is a muscle, and I was going to have to learn how to flex through both small and big moments in order to reclaim my voice. With every conversation and encounter I had, I was tested. The chance to cause a bit of tension in a conversation would come up. I could either hide and laugh it off, or pause, breathe, and state my true opinions.

I started telling people that in fact I did not want to go out to the bar to yell over worn-out pop music. Without shame, I started telling people I love self-help books. I started telling people that I struggle with depression and anxiety, and that I am a survivor of sexual abuse. The reveals were getting deeper and deeper, and I found that I could handle it all. With each moment of flexing my bravery, I felt lighter.

My ability to speak up for myself in real life started to flow into my songwriting and dreams. In fact, I started to have dreams of the younger version of me, saying all the things I had never had the strength to say. One night in particular, I dreamed that my abuser was hitting me, and someone was standing by, watching it all happen. The younger version of me looked up at the observer and said two things I had never said in real life: "I need help. This is wrong."

The observer merely looked on, calmly urging me, "If you say something, you'll make it worse. Just be quiet for now, and it'll be over soon."

The younger version of me then burst out with a quivering yet defiant reply: "I can't keep quiet."

And that is how the chorus of my song "Quiet" came. I woke up the next day feeling stunned by the visceral, powerful dream. I went to my writing session and told my co-writer, AG, about it. She then pointed out that "I can't keep quiet" could be the chorus. Once she said that, the melody and remaining lyrics flooded into my conscious:

I can't keep quiet, no no no
A one woman riot, no no no
I can't keep quiet.

The song was finished in about four hours. It's as if all the lyrics were dripping down from the hands of mother universe, filling the glass jars that AG and I were holding up to the sky.

Something beautiful happened after the song was written: the ball of stuck energy that had weighed heavily in my throat since I was fourteen years old immediately dissipated. I felt like I could finally breathe. The truth shall set you free.

I didn't think my gentle rebel ballad would have a place in a world that preferred up-tempo love songs and bops. My song was not a light summer jam. It was a deep and personal song that stemmed from the trauma of my childhood. Knowing this, I decided that it wouldn't matter where the song ended up, because it had already changed me for the better. I felt as weightless as I had ever felt, and that was priceless.

A YEAR LATER, I watched the map of the United States bleed red on election night of 2016. Again, the flashes of traveling heat coursed through me. This time, I paid attention to the feeling. The traveling heat was the same sensation I had felt when I dreamed about defiantly saying "I can't keep quiet."

I decided to take action by sharing this song to honor all the women gathering in D.C. On the day of the Women's March, twenty-five strangers and I met among the dense sea of human beings wearing pink pussy hats. We harmonized and sang "Quiet" together.

During our last performance of the day, a woman by the name of Alma Ha'rel walked by and filmed us. The video she posted on her social media accounts amassed fourteen million views over the next two days. In response to this unexpected visibility, I decided to upload my sheet music and recordings for free to the public. I told them that they too could sing. Thousands of people downloaded the sheet music, and a few weeks later, choirs from all over the world were flash-mobbing the song. Sweden. Ghana. Australia. Hong Kong. Japan . . .

I watched with awe as these people from all over the world echoed back to me their own stories of pain and survival through my lyrics. Following my traveling heat led me to a global family, reminding me that I was not alone.

I stay close to my inner knowing now, as I allow for that traveling heat to guide me back to myself, time and time again. No matter how disruptive my life choices and truths are to the status quo, I continue to develop my own justice voice by lovingly, yet candidly, stating my truths. As Brené Brown says, "Clarity is kindness."

I don't regret that dark time in my life. In fact, this trauma is what has shaped my appreciation for my truth, and I am using my voice to amplify it. We turn our pain into power. Into passion. Into purpose. Into progress.

Almost on a daily basis, I thank that fourteen-year-old version of me for waiting for me to return to her.

The most beautiful thing is that she welcomed me with warm, open arms when I did. I no longer trivialize intimacy. I honor myself by trying to create deep and authentic relationships, because I know that's what fourteen-year-old me would want.

FLYING FREE

JILLIAN MERCADO

I IMAGINE MANY PEOPLE SHARE MY FEAR OF FLYING, but I'd also guess it's for a very different reason. I think people are mostly scared of planes crashing—clutching the armrest when turbulence hits, or at takeoff and landing. For me, there is the very real fear that in the process of traveling and flying I am going to lose my freedom.

I've been traveling since an extremely young age. Every summer, we would visit family in the Dominican Republic. I vividly remember the joy and sheer anticipation I would feel leading up to each trip. Through my young eyes, I saw leaving the United States as traveling to another world. The plane was a rocket ship taking me away to another planet. The only thing getting in the way of my grand adventure was the airport.

Airports were a major obstacle. Particularly back then, but even still today, airports were not very advanced when it came to accessibility.

There was always extra attention around me when we would arrive at the airport—and not the good kind. The kind that makes you feel like a burden. The first big inconvenience was that I would have to switch to my manual wheelchair instead of my electric wheelchair, because a place like the Dominican Republic wasn't a good place to bring an expensive chair. Switching chairs meant giving up the majority of my independence. When I was in that chair, I couldn't do anything on my own. Something that seems as basic as using the restroom would be a multi-step process requiring significant assistance.

Then there would be the way people at the airport would always talk over me. Even now, when I can speak up for myself, people still tend to talk over me. Back then, they'd mostly talk to my mom instead. I don't think my family even considered asking my opinion; they thought it was necessary for them to be my voice in order to get my needs met.

On one trip, after we landed in the Dominican Republic, I was immediately grouped with the other people who needed assistive devices, as we are always last off the aircraft. My chair would be the last thing unpacked, after the luggage, a process that could take fifteen to twenty minutes at the fastest, and sometimes up to an hour. This time it seemed to take forever. As I waited with my family, I felt totally worthless. Can you imagine waiting for your assistive device for over an hour after everyone else has left the plane? This time I decided to speak up and ask the flight attendants if there was any way the process could move along more quickly, but as I started to speak, my sister asked me to stop. She was worried the flight attendants wouldn't know how to deal with me being so outspoken, since the other people with disabilities seemed to be fine with the wait. People with disabilities like me are used to doing what we're told and not causing a scene or asking questions. I understood why my sister wanted me to be silent, even though I was filled with frustration, and I stopped asking.

I would sometimes try to explain to my family that although I knew they were well-intentioned, I wanted to be able to speak on my own behalf in these situations, because at the end of the day it was my body and my life. The way others talked about me instead of to me made me feel small, like my thoughts, feelings, and preferences were somehow invalid. "If they knew how belittling this felt," I would think, "they would understand that this is a big deal for me." But people still tended to address my mom or other family members instead of me, and for the most part I let it go, not wanting to make the situation more complicated than it already was. I would swallow my words and keep it moving, understanding that traveling was already very overwhelming for all of us. My mom had taught me to always speak up on my own behalf, yet when there were so many circumstances and variables to deal with and it wasn't necessarily easy for me to get my needs met—which was especially the case at airports—she would take the wheel. I think we both figured that getting the job done was more important than who did the asking. What we didn't consider was how I would have to fight this fight on my own every single time I would travel as an adult.

Now I often travel by myself, so it's completely up to me to ask for what I need. And what I've seen is that airlines will often attempt to take advantage of me because they think I'm not smart enough or won't dare to speak up for myself. There was an occasion when I flew to California, landing at about 11 P.M. I was the last one on the plane as usual, waiting for my wheelchair. Fifteen minutes went by. No sign of my chair. I wasn't feeling very well that day and was in no rush at all, so I let them take their time. When another twenty-five minutes passed, I decided to ask a nearby flight attendant for an update, and she told me something I'd heard countless times before: "You need to be patient. These things take a while." Normally I would keep quiet and try to be patient, like I always did, but this time all the moments I had not spoken up seemed to come rushing back to me at once. "It isn't my fault that this is taking so long," I thought. "It's not fair. I shouldn't be treated this way due to poor planning on the airline's part." Before this day, I had never understood why so many people with disabilities felt angry, but now I could see how constantly being disregarded and disrespected had taken a toll on me, too. An image of me as a child flying to the Dominican Republic came into my mind, and I decided that from now on, I wanted to do everything within my power to make my younger self proud.

"It's unacceptable that I have been waiting over half an hour for my chair," I told the flight attendant, "and I want to speak to a manager immediately." She seemed taken aback, but hurried off to find her boss. I soon found out that my chair had just been hanging out in a nearby hallway without anyone realizing it was there or standing guard to make sure it wasn't damaged or taken. From that day on, I resolved to always speak up. My freedom—which my chair provides me—is too precious to lose.

I travel with constant fear that my chair might be damaged or even lost by the airline. This is a very real fear. One time an airline snapped my chair into three pieces. When I tried to investigate what happened, it was a constant blame game, never any answers. They weren't treating my chair as the necessity and freedom that it is.

The truth is, I lose my freedom every time I board a

plane. There have been many times where I am sitting in the window seat, watching the cargo staff attempt to load my chair onto the plane on the luggage belt alongside the other luggage without protection on either side. With one false move, my chair could fall sideways and break. Thankfully my chair has never completely fallen off the luggage belt, but that should not have to be something I worry about every single time I fly. Each time it feels like a nightmare that I can't wake up from. I'm trusting the airline with my most valuable possession, the key to my freedom, yet I've seen them treat strollers and musical equipment with more care. I've had multiple conversations with managers, and time and time again they deny what I can see with my own eyes, make excuses, and repeat that all their employees receive intensive training. It's clear to me that the training is not done by people who have a disability.

I recently researched how often airlines mishandle or damage assistive devices, and found that it happens on average twenty-four times a year. It breaks my heart that this affects so many people and can become the reason why they don't fly. There are so many people who want to travel and experience the world but don't because they can't afford to risk having to buy a new chair. As people with disabilities, we have to ask ourselves, "Am I going to enjoy this trip or will I have to spend two months waiting to get my chair back?"

When airlines break or damage an assistive device, it usually takes a minimum of two months for it to get fixed by either the manufacturer of the wheelchair or a third-party repair company hired by the airport. We have no control over the wait time because pieces need to be ordered, protocols have to be followed, and insurance needs to approve. We usually can't just go to a repair shop in our cities, like when a car breaks down.

In order to protect my freedom and use the calm, strong voice my younger self always hoped I could have, I created a system of reminders and tricks that I use when I fly—and it's a system I try to remember any time I'm in a position of powerlessness and fear.

1. *Know my rights.* I have the right to ask for help, and the right to refuse it. There are things I can't do on my own, and there are things I am capable of doing alone. I also have the right to ask to speak to a manager if I'm not getting the answers I need or the respect I deserve.

2. *Take responsibility.* I can't assume others understand my situation—the capabilities of my device, the way it works, and its importance—so I make sure I have all that information, down to the weight and dimensions of my chair, and communicate it patiently and consistently. I might sometimes feel like a parakeet, repeating and repeating how to handle my chair, but nothing should hap-

pen without my consent. When I'm flying, I can ask for a window seat and record the loading of my chair into the plane in order to document any mishandling.

3. *Know what to expect.* I find that when I remind myself beforehand that it's going to take at least twenty minutes for the airline to find my chair, I can endure that twenty minutes much more easily. If I set up a different expectation for myself, the frustration sets in.

4. *Breathe.* When I'm frustrated, I have to remember that yelling or being rude does not help the situation. Each time I fly, for example, I have to wait an extra fifteen minutes at security for a TSA agent to pat me down, and I hear the same speech about the pat-down each time. I do a lot of breathing exercises to reduce my anxiety and increase my patience.

My life has always been about survival and calculated risk, whether it's trusting someone to help me put my shoes on or flying under circumstances where disability isn't understood in the way it should be. Now it's also about believing in the power of my own voice. I want to live in a world where people with disabilities are humanized. Where airlines treat an assistive device like a valuable passenger, not like any other piece of luggage. Until that happens, I will continue fighting—by asking for what I need, calling out issues when they arise, and holding others accountable. I know what it's like to stay quiet and I know what it's like to use my voice. I choose my worthiness and freedom. I choose to speak up.

MY FUNNY VALENTINE

MAYSOON ZAYID

VALENTINE'S DAY. THE HOLIDAY CREATED BY HALL-mark to taunt all the single ladies, the loveless lads, and the unattached nonbinaries.

I am not a fan of VD and I never have been. My oldest sister was born on Cupid's favorite holiday, so for as long as I can remember, February 14 was about celebrating her. If it was up to my mom, she would have skipped the hearts and candy altogether. My father, however, insisted on buying her flowers and something sparkly. My folks were definitely not the type to Valentine their kids, so the rest of us got nothing.

When I got to kindergarten, Valentine's Day became super-stressful. I was raised in a Muslim family. We were four girls, and liking boys was strictly forbidden. My parents didn't mind that we studied and socialized with the guys, but Valentine's cards would be crossing the line, even at the age of five. If we wanted to participate, we could hand a greeting to any gal. Handing just half the class cards would have been fine by me—I have cerebral palsy and scrawling twenty-five students' names on tiny greetings was super-challenging. Sadly, that was not an option. My kindergarten teacher had rules. It was all or nothing. If you didn't have cards for everyone, then no one would get one. I petitioned my teacher to make an exception due to my faith, but she would not budge. She laughed in my face and said hell no.

Kindergarten wasn't all that bad. I gave nothing, but I still got tons of cards, candy, and even a red Beanie Baby bear. First grade wasn't such a picnic. My fellow students would begrudgingly hand me a Hershey's kiss and then stare me down, knowing I would not reciprocate. By the seventh grade, I figured out that I could give out my Valentines behind my overlords' backs. I existed before social media. No one was going to snitch on me or post me. I made my greetings by hand. My CP made me shake all the time. I had no business cutting loose-leaf paper into hearts. I risked my digits just to be included.

By high school, we were no longer forced to pretend we loved everyone. We could pick and choose the objects of our affection. Being a teen comes with its own angst. Mine came in the form of my high school's annual Valentine's Day fundraiser. The student council would sell handmade paper carnations. Volunteers, including myself, spent months twisting pipe cleaners around tissue paper and creating thousands of red, pink, and white flowers. Each color had a meaning. Red was love, white was friendship, and pink was sexy. This was many moons ago and people had no idea what age-appropriate was.

The flowers were distributed on Valentine's Day in homeroom. I wanted nothing to do with the pink flowers. If I had gotten one, I would've tossed it in the trash. Crushing on Danny Biroc behind my parents' backs was one thing, but bringing home a sexy bloom would have gotten my Muslim butt grounded for life. From freshman to senior year, I would always get a bouquet of white roses. I had had the same gaggle of girlfriends since kindergarten. I loved them, they loved me, and we forked out the money to prove it. White is nice, but everyone wants at least one red stem. This wasn't Galentine's Day, where we celebrate our best buds. This was Valentine's Day, and every commercial that I was subjected to for the first fourteen days of February reminded me that if the love wasn't romantic, it simply did not count.

The only thing worse than being red-rose-less was having no blooms at all. Each homeroom had a couple of heartbroken young adults who hadn't received a single sprig. I remember twisting together my seven carnations while the flowerless child next to me stared blankly at the chalkboard. Those sad students stuck with me. I finally realized why all or nothing was required in grammar school.

My senior year, I was elected student council president. One of my campaign promises was that no teen would go roseless again. I kept my word and made sure that every single soul in Cliffside Park High School got at least one white rose. That same Valentine's Day, I decided to defy my masters. I snuck out with my first love. My date took me to a stand-up comedy show. Armed with fake IDs, we got front-row seats. I nervously laughed the night away, with visions of my father catching me holding hands with a boy at a comedy club dancing through my head.

Perhaps it is my karma for defying my parents all those years ago: I never went on another Valentine's Day outing. I once bought a dude a car for Christmas and he still picked someone else to be his Valentine. I have been subjected to a slew of weddings on Cupid's day. If you are engaged and planning your nuptials, please keep in mind that only assholes set February 14 as their wedding day. It is bad enough that you throw bowling-ball-sized bouquets at single women's heads. Making them try to find a wedding date on Valentine's Day is a mean girl's move.

For years, I was chronically Valentine-less, but I refused to stop believing, and my quest led me to one of my greatest loves of all. I had just graduated from college and was chilling at the Barnes & Noble in Lincoln Center because I was jobless. It was my favorite spot in Manhattan due to its proximity to the New York City Ballet and the high school where the movie *Fame* was set. I dreamed of being a contestant on *Jeopardy!* so I spent my ample free time memorizing a potpourri of trivia.

I was lounging in an overstuffed chair, perusing a book on defunct maps of the Middle East, when my studies were interrupted. The most beautiful boy I ever did see strolled by me. I tossed aside the atlas and began to pursue him. My plan was to stumble across his path so that we could meet-cute like in a romantic comedy. This would also give me an opening to nonchalantly mention my disability. I needed to get in front of the object of my desire, but this babe walked briskly. I had to zigzag across the street like Frogger just to keep up with him.

He entered a building, and of course I followed. He held the door for me, and we waited for the elevator in silence. Due to my CP, standing is not my thing. I can dance, I can walk in heels, but if I'm upright for more than a second, I topple over. I leaned on the wall next to the elevator door, trying to look sexy while avoiding crumpling to the ground. My eyes locked with a pair of bright blue peepers staring back at me from a painted mural. It was Jesus Christ, and this was his Church of Latter-day Saints. A loud ding snapped me out of my trance. My mystery man and I rode the elevator up silently together. Like a lemming, I followed him into a Bible study class. He took a seat, and I plopped down right next to him. He charmingly offered to share his holy book with me, since I was Bible-less. Muslim me didn't want to be rude, so I said, "Amen!"

The class lasted an eternity. It was like the never-ending story. When it finally finished, a tall, stunning, blue-eyed Barbie sidled up to us. She introduced herself as Alyee and handed me a printed-out flyer inviting me to her birthday party. She had just finished her mission and was spending a gap year in New York City before heading to law school. Alyee invited everyone in the Bible study class, including me. I had a flashback to the kindergarten Valentine's Day rule—either everyone gets a card or no one does. It was what Jesus would do. The dude sitting next to me said he was in, which meant I was in too.

I went to Alyee's birthday party, and she became my best friend in the world. I have always been blessed with amazing friendships with women. I am still friends with the seven girls who used to send me white roses in homeroom, but I had always dreamed of finding a man to complete me. That all changed the day that I met Allyson Russell Snow. Alyee was born in Idaho, was raised in Florida, and went to college in Montana. Upon graduating, she headed out on a Mormon mission. She served in the Spanish-speaking district of

San Francisco. Once her mission was accomplished, she landed in New York City, where she found me. I have met a lot of extremely religious people, being from the Holy Land and all, but I have never met anyone more Jesus-like than Alyee. For a year we slayed NYC. It was like *Sex and the City* without the sex. Muslims and Mormons have a lot in common—we're not supposed to drink, and no doing the wild thing before marriage. Hanging out with Alyee made it very easy for me to stick to my unwanted values. Like Danny and Sandy at the end of summer in *Grease*, we were torn asunder when autumn came.

Alyee left the big city for law school in our nation's capital. We would alternate weekends in D.C. and New York. It was all fun and games until Brigham Young University gave Alyee an offer she couldn't refuse. She abandoned the East Coast for the great Salt Lake. I assumed I would never see her again. This was before cellphones and Facebook. If your bestie moved to another state, it was pretty much the equivalent of being dead. I am terrible at long-distance relationships, but Alyee was the queen of keeping in touch. She is also the poster child for ride-or-die friendship. If I ever find myself in lockup, Alyee is undoubtedly my one phone call.

While Alyee was studying for the bar exam, I was falling in love with a Broadway star. Zeph was a River-dancer. My parents couldn't afford physical therapy, so they sent me to tap class. Riverdancing is like tapping except you don't move your arms. I had always dreamed of dancing on Broadway. Dating a member of the chorus line was the next best thing. Anytime Alyee found the quarters and a payphone to dial me, I would regale her with stories of my fairy-tale relationship. But there was no happy ending. In the end, the Riverdancer clog-danced on my heart.

Alyee dropped her life and flew to New Jersey. This was my first real heartbreak and I dealt with it like one of my beloved soap divas. I was sloppy. Alyee scooped me up and tossed me into my gold Jeep Grand Cherokee, and we drove cross-country to Utah so that she could bring me back to full yay! I was a substitute teacher, so I definitely had the time.

Alyee and I took ride-or-die to a whole new level because we seriously almost lost our lives on the heartbreak road trip. If we had followed Route 80 west without detouring, we would have been just fine. But like a cat, Alyee was easily distracted. In Indiana, she saw a drive-through corn maze and had to give it a whirl. I am a person of color, I know what happens to us in horror movies. It's always the silly white girl who goes racing into harm's way, and that is exactly what Alyee did. We got lost in the maze for four and a half hours. The Cherokee was on its last drop of gas when a yellow Corvette entered the field and began stalking us. We had no GPS and no cellphones. My Jersey girl instincts kicked in. I was done with lefts and rights. I drove straight ahead, mowing down the corn, so I could break on through to the other side. To this day, I am amazed that we were not serial-killed.

Our trip was poorly planned, and halfway through, Alyee realized she would have to fly home from Kentucky so as not to miss the bar exam. I dropped her off at the Louisville airport, which would someday bear the name of Muhammad Ali, and she said she would pray for me to make it to Utah alive. I should've turned back to Jersey, but instead I rolled on out of Kentucky, through Missouri, and into Kansas. Before she abandoned me, Alyee had taught me that I could survive without a love interest and that I could get by with a little help from my friend. After she flew off into the sunset, I discovered something even more important: I could make it on my own.

I am sure that Kansas is a lovely place, but its stretch of Interstate 70 is mind-numbing. On my solo road trip, there was only one thing to look at—countless billboards that read "X Miles to the World's Largest Prairie Dog!" These signs counted down the miles to Prairie Dog Town by fifties, tens, and then, finally, singles. For five hundred miles I waited to see this rodent of an unusually large size. It is good to have goals other than getting hitched. When I finally got there, the prairie dog wasn't even alive. It was taxidermied. I leaned up against it and took what might have been the world's first selfie with a disposable camera that Alyee had left with me to document the rest of my journey.

I was GPS-less and had nothing but printed-out MapQuest directions to guide me. Miraculously, I made it to the land of milk and honey. Upon my arrival in Utah, I learned that my lousy luck with love had rubbed off on my best friend. Alyee had suffered her own bad breakup. The Mormon club owner she had planned to wed had dumped her, and she was determined to win him back. Using her substantial connections in the singles ward at her church, she managed to score us an invite to her ex's annual Thanksgiving potluck.

Depressed me was the perfect wingchick. Instead of trying to talk Alyee out of getting back her former man, I cheered her on with the type of zeal that only a special kid could muster. We had a strategy. Anytime I saw her ex, Cliff, the host of the soiree, canoodling with any other person, I would break up the banter by asking them to tell Muslim me more about the Church of Jesus Christ of Latter-day Saints. Every person at the party wanted a shot at saving my soul. As Alyee and Cliff reconnected over mashed potatoes and gravy, I sat surrounded by my new Christ-adoring admirers. I told them the tale of how the Riverdancer had ravaged my heart, and they laughed hysterically. My greatest pain brought inexplicable joy to my newfound friends. I had always been a drama queen. That day, I discovered that comedy was a much better fit for me. I drove east on Route 80 and headed back to Jersey. When I got back home safe and sound, I made a beeline for Broadway. I limped into Carolines Comedy Club and signed up for my very first stand-up class.

On the same day that I discovered my destiny, Alyee's fate was also sealed. She reunited with Cliff, they got married, and now they have five children. Alyee passed the bar with flying colors and represents the meek in court so that they can inherit the earth. She juggles it all, yet still finds time for me. She attended my TED Talk, she was one of my bridesmaids, and she flew to Jersey for my first book cover shoot. She is my own personal Jesus, and anytime I need her, she is by my side.

I may never have another funny Valentine, and that's fine by me. All of those Valentine's Day commercials I was force-fed over the decades of my life were wrong. You don't need somebody to put a ring on it. I am happy to die alone and be eaten by my cat, and I am blessed and lucky to know that Alyee or one of her many offspring will make sure that doesn't happen.

WAKE UP, LOVE

BOZOMA SAINT JOHN

BEEP.

SOMEWHERE BETWEEN DREAMS and wakefulness, I reach out toward my nightstand, where my phone alarm is screaming angrily at me to wake up. It is incessant and disturbing my hard-won peace. I'm trying to put my finger on where I am and what I'm doing here, knowing that it couldn't have been that long ago when I finally drifted off. In the corner of my mind I'm trying to remember something lost in the sleepiness that has enveloped me, but I can't grasp it. Notes of lavender swirl around my senses; I inhale deeply, grateful for the familiarity and comfort. Ah. I'm at home. Safe. I stab at the screen with sleepy force, pleading with a searching fingertip for the snooze button.

SILENCE.

MY EYES WON'T obey my command to open, but my ears are on high alert. I'm listening intently for the heartbeat next to me. And I wish mine wouldn't beat so loudly in my own ears. Shhhhh. I can't hear anything. My terror starts to accelerate as my searching fingertips inch toward the other side of my California-king bed. It's empty. Why? What? How? When? My eyes fly open in shock. But, a second later, the answering memories rush in. Pain overcomes the terror, starting at the back of my throat and stifling the sob that wishes to escape. When people say they feel choked up, is this the feeling they mean? I want to cry out but there is a vise-like grip on my insides, shutting down all function. It would be easier to succumb to the pain, to sink into the darkness from which I just woke. But I can't do that today. Today I have to get up. I have to get up like the other 2,251 days that I've woken up after the morning Peter died.

BAM.

BY SHEER WILL, I fling the comforter off my body, allowing the cool air of my room to caress my body into alertness. The air is as cool as the other side of the bed, and it's a visceral reminder that I am alone. Alone. Alone though I don't wish to be. Alone though my heart aches in these small hours of the day when no one else moves. But I find that the aloneness isn't as bad when it seems as if no one else in the world is stirring. If I hold my breath, I hear nothing at all, and in that nothingness the world is quiet. I don't have to hear the beginnings of everyone else's bustling, coupled lives. But my spirit starts to fight against my rib cage because holding my breath hurts almost more than breathing. I have no peace in my nothingness. So I breathe in my singular breaths, calming my racing heart, which threatens to explode under the pressure of its sadness.

BEEP.

I'M STARTLED BY that damn alarm, which is screaming again. But I let it ring for a bit longer, as the sound fills the lonely space and adds life to my too-quiet room. It's also reminding me that I must stand up. I must move forward. In that way, I welcome the cacophony that invades my peace upon waking every day. The battle is in my heart; I fight between curling inward to ward off the pain that threatens to consume my whole being and the desire to seek out new meaning in this life I'm now living. I've always been an optimist. I'm the one who knows everything will be okay even in the face of a dark journey because I search for a faint light in the distance. But the light was turned off at the end of the tunnel on the day the oncologist said Peter's life would come to an end sooner than we expected. On that day, my optimism failed me. I thrashed against the promise of new dawns and hopeful joy in the adventure of life's endless days. I careened toward the fear of a span of years in which I'd have to raise our daughter alone. Today, like yesterday and tomorrow, I must make an active choice to get up.

THUD.

MY FEET TINGLE as they hit my cool hardwood floor and blood rushes through my sluggish limbs. What will I do today? The question has had the dual purpose of haunting and motivating me ever since Peter and I started to count down the days until his death. We'd get up and set an intention for our action that day. Should we do something playful? Something meaningful? Something practical? Something that I found in my dreams? The practice has been hard to break in the days since December 11, 2013, when we stopped doing it together. If I lose this practice, I will not just have lost his physical presence, I will have lost him altogether. So I ask myself that same question each morning, as if he's here and we can decide together how we will engage the world today. I search my mind for the answer, knowing that my schedule is already packed to the brim: conference calls, lunch meeting, strategy review, bestie debrief about her new guy, etc. Sometimes I wonder if I stay so busy in order to keep myself from having to decide what to do without him. It's easier to fill my time with obligations that feel outside of my control so that I don't have to make a choice. I have given everyone else the power to make my life a blur of movement.

FLICK.

THE BATHROOM LIGHT burns my eyes as I rub them to gain focus. I look at the woman looking at me. I'm 2,251 days older than the day my life shifted on its axis. There are new gray hairs at my crown. There are a few more wrinkles in my squint as I scrutinize myself. I turn to the left to look at my body profile. It's not so bad. I've been working on it to erase the doubt that anyone will want to feel my intimate strength again. I rip off the old college T-shirt that I sleep in to get a better look. I flex in the mirror, admiring the new lines of definition. They scream strength. But I feel vulnerable. I don't know how to fill the void in my heart. I'm longing for comfort and love, but they escape me. There are not enough reps of bicep curls or lunges or sit-ups I can do to force love back into my life. I know it must come willingly and perhaps unexpectedly. But I'm impatient. I want love again NOW. I want it in this moment of doubt as I stare at myself. The fears that threaten to send me crying back under the sheets sit on the tip of my tongue, but I'm afraid to speak them aloud. Will I ever find love again? Will I become so accustomed to my loneliness that I forget what intimacy feels like? Am I too independent for another man to find himself in the unasked question in my gaze? If these questioning fears are spoken, will they become true? We are all powerful enough to control our destiny through the language we use to commune with ourselves. I know that. I also know that I'm scared. I want love but I don't want to lose it again. Should my intentions today be to find my way to love?

RING!

I PICK UP my phone as it alerts me with the first notification of the day. I open my calendar. It's full. There's no time to find love today, but perhaps it will find me. Ahhhhh. There's that optimism. Maybe it's not gone. Maybe it's just hidden, afraid to show itself in the light of the uncertainty of life. Nothing in my life has gone according to my plans, so maybe today isn't going to be what I think it's going to be, either. But would I want it to be predictable? I've gone to psychics and mediums and horoscopes to tell my future, but I haven't found my peace there, either. I come away from those experiences yearning for more information, more connection, and more certainty. There are no answers to be found outside of myself. My actions determine my future regardless of what destiny throws my way. I look at the mirror and into my brown eyes, which change from light to dark depending on my mood. I steel myself and command: Bozoma, be open to expanding your heart and stepping into love today.

LUCY, FULL OF LIFE

GEENA ROCERO

MY BARE FEET DUG INTO THE WARM WHITE SAND beaches of Palawan, Philippines. It was the last few days of a vacation I'd taken with friends from all over the world. A voice from the bamboo beach bar called out, "Gin and tonic is ready!" Each night, my friends and I would watch the sunset in front of our beach cottages, appreciating the opportunity to spend precious time together.

Then I heard a message come through my phone. It was from one of my dear friends back in San Francisco: *Did you hear what happened to Lucy?* It was the kind of message that nobody ever wants to receive.

Heart racing, I typed back, *Please tell me.*

Lucy had a massive stroke and is in a coma at San Francisco General Hospital.

I looked up, two contradicting realities right in front of my eyes. On the one hand, a peaceful and colorful sunset glimmering across the sea. On the other, the dark and panicked feeling of wanting to wake up from a nightmare. I did not know what to do. My friends wrapped me in hugs and words of comfort, giving me the immediate support I needed. Then I decided: the moment I landed back in New York City, I would get on another plane, right away, to go be with Lucy.

Two days later, I found myself standing next to Lucy's hospital bed, looking at her unresponsive body, tubes spilling out of her brain. I massaged her left hand, hoping she could feel my touch. The whole left side of her body was paralyzed. I felt overwhelmed by uncertainty and fear, but also by love. I didn't know if she would recover, but one thing was very clear: the person in front of me, barely clinging to life, had given me more than I could ever repay.

I'd looked up to Lucy since I was fifteen years old. She was on top of her game, very popular, and would win most pageants—which is a big deal, because pageants are considered the national sport of the Philippines. We love pageants and we love our beauty queens. In the month of May, there's a trans pageant almost every day. I dreamed that one day I could be like her.

As I began to participate in transgender beauty pageants myself, Lucy and I met through mutual friends.

These pageants were the way we found our chosen families. We had trans mothers who became both mentors and managers. We had trans sisters who were our competitors onstage but with whom we shared meals during every post-pageant celebration. Joining pageants gave us the opportunity to claim our space in a society that didn't want us to succeed. I learned what it was like to feel empowered and feminine onstage, and how important it was to have humor and a strong sense of self. I would find these traits to be equally as useful as a young transgender immigrant in the United States.

When I was eighteen, I moved to the United States to be with my mom, my cousins, and my grandma. Everything was new. The streets of Vallejo, California—a suburb an hour outside of San Francisco—were clean, the crosswalks were weirdly super-organized, and the air smelled fresh compared to the urban smog of Manila. Despite the beauty around me, I was very scared to start my new life. I was going to be starting from scratch.

A week after I arrived, I pulled out a notebook that had only one thing written in it: Lucy's telephone number. Lucy had moved to San Francisco three years before me and was the only person outside of my family who I knew in the entire country.

"Hey," I said nervously. "I'm here now and I would love to see you."

"Come to San Francisco!" Lucy shouted back with excitement. It was as if she had been waiting for my call, ready to provide the most welcoming spirit that any new immigrant in a new country could hope for.

"How do I get there?" I asked. She suggested I either take a bus to a train or take the ferry. Given that I was completely unfamiliar with how things ran and the seemingly complicated train instructions, I opted for the simple ferry ride. That Friday afternoon, I left carrying only a backpack and an excitement that I could barely contain. At the time, the only thing I knew about San Francisco was that it was home to the Golden Gate Bridge. Forty minutes later, there it was: the Golden Gate Bridge, in real life, shimmering in the intermittent sunlight, patchy fog hovering just above it.

After a short cab ride from the ferry station, I found myself in the hallway outside her apartment door. I could hear Aaliyah's "Try Again" blasting through the walls. When I knocked, she opened the door right away, giving me a big hug with a makeup brush in one hand. "We're going out!" she announced. Though I hadn't seen her for more than three years, she greeted me as if we'd seen each other just yesterday.

As we got dressed in her tiny apartment, next to her bunk bed, she asked, "What jobs are you interested in?"

"Anything," I said.

Excited, she suggested that I find a cosmetics department to work in, where I could sell and apply makeup. This worried me. In the pageants, all I had to do was show up—I had my own dedicated hair and makeup artist and my own fashion stylist.

"You will be just fine," Lucy assured me. "I'll teach you everything."

Lucy and I ended up going to a club called Divas that night, in a neighborhood between lower Nob Hill and the Tenderloin. It was one of her regular spots and she seemed to know everyone there, from the person at the door to the owner. Most importantly, she introduced me to her transgender sisters, who were also from the Philippines. The dance floor was soon filled with these new friends. It almost felt like the whole trans Filipina community in San Francisco was there to welcome me to America. I felt showered with love. We danced for hours, ending up at a twenty-four-hour Thai noodle soup restaurant at 5 A.M.

The following day, Lucy and I started planning how I could get a cosmetics job. It was either Macy's or Nordstrom, she told me. The prospect of finding a job was both exciting and nerve-racking. I was worried that my thick Filipino accent would be a hindrance during a job interview. Lucy confided that I reminded her of when she'd first started out, and she encouraged me to try anyway. She spent the rest of the day teaching me how to apply a decent eye shadow, how to pick the right lipstick, and, most importantly, the proper way to contour a face. She was training me not just for a potential job, but for my own purposes—trying to help me become more familiar with my own face and find out what worked best for me. I learned the power of subtlety in applying makeup, how I could highlight my eyes, lips, and cheeks so I'd look good even in bright sunlight.

On Sunday, we went for Filipino brunch at Max Restaurant in Daly City, also known as "Little Manila," a short car ride away from San Francisco. The trans sisters that Lucy had introduced me to at the club joined us for garlic fried rice, cured pork, and a tamarind-based chicken vegetable soup. In just one weekend, I started to feel like I might be able to find success and belonging in my new life in the United States—and it was all thanks to Lucy. My mom lit up when I came home bursting with stories about everything Lucy had done for me, especially my newfound friends and community.

Now, though, Lucy—always so animated and full of passion—was completely still, lying between the whooshing ventilator and the flashing, beeping heart rate monitor. I wanted her to know how much she meant to me, how grateful I felt for all she'd done for me. Over the next few days, I was tasked with giving updates to our friends in the Philippines. Her nurses told me that the swelling in her brain remained the same and that the only thing we could do was wait.

One of her doctors explained that they were still doing tests, but they thought she might be partially conscious, able to hear what was going on around her. Our friends wanted to video-chat with her, hoping she could hear their messages, that something would change. Our hearts were breaking, but we needed one another and Lucy needed us. Each time someone called, we were scared that this might be the last one.

"What do you remember most about Lucy?" I would ask our friends. I'd turn the volume up high, desperately wanting her to know that her friends were with her. Maybe, together, our love could wake her up.

One night, toward the end of visiting hours, the sounds of the machines started to feel hypnotic, as if Lucy and I were both slowly disappearing. Searching for a dose of hope, I found a video online of one of Lucy's performances in a major trans pageant. It had been broadcast on television, and it happened to be the first time I'd seen Lucy on TV, years before I started joining pageants myself. Performing Janet Jackson's "Together Again," Lucy, surrounded by backup dancers, was wearing a short red dress, her long black hair flowing. She was full of life—exactly the way I wanted to remember her. Overwhelmed with emotion, I decided to play it for her. I placed the phone next to her ear and turned up the volume so that she'd be able to hear over the eerie sounds of the machines. Caught up in the moment, I began singing along, softly at first, then louder as I started to dance as well. When the video stopped, I played it again, then again, then again.

Partway through the fifth rendition, I stopped dancing to take a closer look at Lucy's face. To my shock, I saw tears falling from the corners of her eyes. I started to cry, too, and hugged her tightly. *She can hear the music,* I thought through my sobs. *Maybe she can even hear me singing along.* I had to believe that some part of Lucy was right there with me, inspired to fight back.

A nurse walked in the room and I excitedly shared what had just happened. I showed her the video and pointed to Lucy's wet eyes. The nurse looked surprised to find out that the woman with the short red dress and beautiful long legs was the same person lying there in front of us. I couldn't stop crying. I was flying back to New York the next day and felt desperate for the nurses and doctors to see Lucy as I saw her: not just a patient, but a person brimming over with love, energy, and affection, ready to welcome a near-stranger into her city, community, and life. It wasn't enough to just inspire Lucy—I wanted to inspire *them,* too.

Two weeks later, Lucy regained consciousness. I cried tears of gratitude and relief when I got the news, though I understood that it would be a long road to recovery. She would need to stay in the hospital for two more months before being transferred to a long-term rehabilitation center. All of us—her trans Filipina sisters, her chosen family—would need to work to-gether to make sure she was supported throughout the process. I visited as often as I could.

A few months ago, I took Lucy shopping in down-town San Francisco, pushing her wheelchair in front of me. Her makeup, which she's learned to apply with one hand, was flawless. As we looked through racks of clothing, laughing together, it felt just like our very first day together, when I'd anxiously taken the ferry to her little apartment. Easy. Joyful. Openhearted. Warm. I couldn't imagine what my first few weeks in the United States would have been like without her, and I couldn't imagine a world without her now, either. She is family.

As we exited a store, Lucy suggested we record a live video together so that we could show our friends back home in the Philippines a yellow top she'd just picked out. But I knew it wasn't just about the shirt. This video, us giggling together, having fun, connecting with our community—it was proof that Lucy was still here, still moving forward, still committed to joy. Even now, she was still showing me the way.

CHOOSING LOVE

NKOSINGIPHILE MABASO

I WAS JUST TEN YEARS OLD WHEN MY MOTHER LEFT. The day started like any other: My mother woke up, made food, and cleaned. After bathing, she told me she was going to the store and that she would be back shortly. I remember being sad because I wanted to accompany her, but she insisted that she was going alone. My mother did not return from the store that day. She did not return for two years.

My heart was shattered. At the end of each night, I would sleep with the hope that my mom would return tomorrow. But tomorrow did not come for a long time. Although my mother's disappearance was traumatic and heartbreaking, I did not blame or hate her for leaving. Even when I was too young to understand exactly what was happening, I knew that it took immense strength to come out smiling through tears when you have just been beaten up by someone you love. I wanted better for my mother, and I understood that at some point, leaving became the best thing for her.

My mother did not just leave me and my father behind in the small town we lived in outside of Johannesburg. She also left my fourteen-year-old brother, my seven-year-old little sister, my two-year-old little brother, and my youngest little brother, who was around six months old at the time. My dad, being a traditional Zulu man, decided that because I was the oldest daughter in the house, it was my duty to take over my mother's responsibilities. So at ten years old I started raising my three younger siblings and taking care of the family.

A typical day in my ten-year-old life looked something like this: I woke up, soaked the cloths we used as nappies for my youngest brother, made food (if we had any) for my dad and siblings, helped my little sister bathe and get ready for school, took a bath myself, and then walked with my little sister to school. After school, I would start my chores, carrying my little brother on my back. I would clean the house, wash dishes and pots, and then try to figure out dinner. Sometimes I would do chores for my neighbor and she would pay me cash or give me food because she knew my family needed it.

In the two years my mother was gone, my father beat me up almost every day: "Why is the baby crying?" "Why have you not given the baby food?" "Why is the house dirty?" No matter what I did or didn't do, my father would always find a reason to punish me. I experienced all kinds of abuse in that house. I felt unloved. I felt alone. When my father was not beating me up, my nephew, who is a few years older than me, was beating me up, telling me that no one would ever love me. I remember praying to a God I did not really know or understand because I did not know whom else to turn to.

SCHOOL WAS MY refuge. I worked hard because I loved learning. My teachers believed in me and I excelled in my academics. School became the only place where I could be a child, the only place I felt valued and seen. Two years passed in this same way, where school was the only place I had just to myself, where I could be safe and free. One day in the middle of mathematics class, when I was twelve years old, a boy walked in and told my teacher she was needed at the office. Ten minutes later, the same boy came back to my math class.

This time he called for me and told me they needed me at the principal's office too. I had never been called to the principal's office before, ever. I nervously hurried to the office.

When I got there, several of my teachers were waiting for me, including my math teacher. "Call your father and tell him to bring your birth certificate and your past report cards. We're going to help you apply to the Oprah school," one of my teachers said with excitement and urgency. She told me the applications were due that day and we had to hurry.

I watched Oprah Winfrey's show every weekday after school, and I knew she helped thousands of people. I hadn't known, however, that Oprah had a school, and I didn't know if I would be able to afford it. My first thought was, "They probably do not accept poor people like me." A couple of weeks earlier, I had been watching *Oprah* while cleaning my house. I'd cried, feeling hopeless, because I believed if anyone could help me, it would be Oprah Winfrey, but the show was in the United States; there was no way Oprah could help me.

My teachers explained that the Oprah Winfrey Leadership Academy for Girls (OWLAG) was a school created for girls just like me, girls who were intelligent, had leadership qualities, and were driven but didn't have the financial means to obtain a quality education. I was in awe. Suddenly, being helped by Oprah was possible. I had no idea just how much this opportunity would change my life. I wasn't thinking about my long-term future or any bigger goals, but I knew this was the help I had been crying and praying for.

I was twelve years old when I began my journey at OWLAG. The campus was the most beautiful place I had ever seen. I called it my paradise, my happy place. I had endured more than any twelve-year-old was supposed to; I was ready for some good in my life. And OWLAG was that good in my life. I went from living a life of lack and pain to living a life of abundance, a life filled with love. I had spent most of my childhood sleeping on the floor, but at OWLAG I had my own bed and slept on clean white linen. I ate three meals a day and had snacks in between. I knew I was at the right place and I knew that the experience was changing my life for the better. My first day at the Academy, I got to meet and hug Mom Oprah. It sank in that day: This opportunity was about to change the trajectory of my life. Forever.

When people ask me how being at OWLAG was, I always say it was the best six years of my life. It was also the most challenging six years of my life. I didn't feel like I was worthy of the opportunity. I felt too poor. Too fat. Too ugly. For the first few years, I couldn't speak up in front of a group of people without my whole body and voice trembling. Most days I thought it was a mistake that I had ended up there and I was terrified everyone else would realize it too. Away from the turmoil of home, I finally had time to think, to be with myself and process what I had been through. As I conversed with other girls about my childhood, I started getting sad. I was sad because my story made everyone else sad.

Before OWLAG, I had thought I had a normal childhood. I had naively assumed everyone was raising their siblings in some way, that everyone was being "disciplined" in the same way I was at home. It was in the little, constant differences from some of the other girls that I started to realize just how traumatic my childhood had been. When most of my sisters were crying, missing home, I was thinking of how I didn't really want to go back home. When I would tell my story with a smile on my face, I saw that those who were listening would tear up, heartbroken and sad. The more I spoke with the girls who had amazing relationships with their parents, the more I realized how much I longed for a parent's love and guidance.

Only at the Academy did I really start to feel the feelings of abandonment that I'd had no time to feel when my mother left. I realized how afraid I was. Of being rejected. Of being abandoned. I struggled to open up and build genuine connections. I was always afraid to make mistakes in my relationships, with peers and elders alike. I was scared that if I said or did the wrong thing, I would be punished or abandoned. I self-destructed. I left people before they left me. For a while it made me feel empowered. But I didn't yet realize that running from love was running from myself, from all that is beautiful in life. When I tried to avoid the pain, I consequently was avoiding love too.

IN MY FIRST year at OWLAG, I was called into the therapist's office along with some of my sisters. Because of the circumstances at home and what I had gone through, it was suggested that I go to therapy so I could process and begin healing. The first few months of group therapy, I was silent. When asked how I was doing, I would only say I was fine or okay. I always had a pillow on my lap; I used it to cover my face. I was in a safe space, but I was still crippled by fear. I had low self-esteem and no sense of self-worth or self-love. The group was patient and understanding. They let me say "fine" and "okay" as many times as I needed to. They validated and acknowledged my feelings, no matter how complicated or messy they were. To this day, I am grateful for group therapy because it helped me begin to heal.

While at OWLAG and in therapy, I learned to start forgiving my parents and accept the difficult childhood I had. Mom Oprah always says that forgiveness is giving up the hope that the past could have been any different. Once I released what I wished my life could have been like, I was able to fully embrace the miracle and beauty of the life I was living. I was living the life of my wildest dreams. I had residence mothers who loved and guided me like their own. I had teachers who wanted to see me do well, teachers who poured love and life into me. I had friends who did not want me to be anyone else other than myself, even when I thought being myself was a mistake. I could not change the past, and eventually I did not want to. I know now that everything that has happened to me happened *for* me. My childhood was painful. It was shattering. It was traumatizing. But it had beautiful moments. And it helped shape me into a beautiful person.

This journey of healing and accepting ignited a spark in me. Once I was able to talk about my feelings, no one could shut me up. I started learning about myself, and I was always excited to learn more. I wanted to face my pain, to face myself. I learned to be my own home, even when I had no physical building that I called home. And I saw the value of this healing journey. Without romanticizing the trauma, I now understand that it all led me here and I absolutely love it here. I love who I am and who I am constantly becoming. I have more peace. I am more secure in myself. I live more in the moment and try to not get stuck on the past. I don't worry too much about the future anymore because I learned that it will all always be well. No matter what happens.

AFTER OWLAG, I was accepted at Skidmore College in upstate New York. I would not have dared to even apply for such an opportunity had I not had those six years of healing and processing at the Academy. But having done the emotional work, I had parts of me that knew I deserved everything good I wished and longed for. I was able to rise to the occasion. I adjusted well at Skidmore and became an active, engaged member of the community. I had good relationships with students, staff, and faculty alike, and I was on the board of the African Heritage Awareness club. With a friend, I created a band. Again, I saw the value of choosing love. I loved most of my experiences. I loved my friends. I loved my classes. I loved myself. I did not just survive, I thrived.

I know now that my purpose is to choose love. Even when fear creeps in and tries to take over, I choose to love myself and those around me. I choose to love my life as it is. Loving myself has allowed me to make better choices for me instead of making destructive choices out of fear. Now I have hundreds of friends who have become sisters. We hold one another when we experience loss. We dance and celebrate when one of us succeeds. It is beautiful. It is wholesome. It has set the tone for all the beautiful relationships I'll have in the future. And I am better for it.

I choose to share my story to remind myself of how miraculous my journey has been. I choose to share my story to remind people that our circumstances do not define us. When I am in pain, I sometimes get so overwhelmed by it that I start convincing myself the pain will never end. But everything ends. "This too shall pass," I remind myself. The good moments will pass, and I will face another challenge. But while it is good, I enjoy and bask in the goodness. When challenges arise, I remind myself to be grateful for all that is still good in my life and to be grateful for the lessons, even if they are painful or uncomfortable.

The most beautiful part of this journey, for me, has been forgiving my parents. My mother returned home after I started at OWLAG, though we never lived in the same house again. My father unlearned depending on violence to solve all his problems. He learned to sit us down and talk through issues. I stopped seeing my parents as just parents and now see them also as human beings, beings who once had their own childhoods and their own dreams. I have seen and heard about how brutal life has been to my parents. They did not know any better. And although it was chaotic and violent, my parents gave me the best life they knew how.

They went through their trauma and never had the chance to heal, to process. It is true: hurt people hurt people. My parents never hated me, and nothing bad that happened to me was a result of my unworthiness. I had two broken people who loved me and tried their best to show me that they cared. But they couldn't give me a love they did not have. I have been able to have difficult conversations about the past with my parents, and those conversations allowed me and my parents to heal together. Today I am a warrior of love and light. Through my vulnerability and willingness to choose love, I have inspired a positive change within my family. That makes it all worth it. For that, I will be eternally grateful.

WHEN SISTERHOOD ENDS

LUVVIE AJAYI JONES

I GOT MARRIED IN 2019, AND ON THE WAY TO BEING A wife, I dealt with the heartbreak of losing a few friends I thought would be lifelong. One in particular was tough for me to handle. As a deeply loyal, loves-to-plan-out-her-life-and-know-what's-coming Capricorn, change of any type usually jars me. So when I go through change that feels like something is taken away from me, I end up in a cocoon of my own making, singing sad love songs by Toni Braxton. My love songs aren't about losing romantic love, but about losing something that sometimes feels even bigger: the love of (someone you thought was) a lifelong buddy.

Anyone who goes through wedding planning and comes out on the other side not having lost their mind and been committed to an institution is a superhero.

It is life's boot camp. The process teaches you so much about yourself, but it also teaches you a lot about everyone else you know.

Weddings can be the catalyst of a lot of heartbreak, even when you happily marry the one you love, like I did.

I had heard for years that getting married is one of the things that makes people show their whole entire asses with bad behavior. Even though it should be just about the bride and groom, it is often expanded to include everyone else's feelings, from the aunt you wished you didn't have to invite to the high school friends you haven't spoken to in years who somehow expect to make the guest list.

For me, what caused my heartbreak was losing a friend I thought I'd be in rocking chairs with in fifty years, reflecting on our twenties shenanigans and how we used to act up. We'd been friends since college. At one point, we even called each other the so-you-know-it's-real title of "best friends." We'd slept on twin beds together to get through losing boyfriends, been there for each other through post-college living in the big cities of our choice, and eventually became adults trying to figure it out together.

Over the four years before my wedding, we probably spoke every other month or two. Lives get busy, so those were full-on "catch me up on life" conversations. I just knew that in our olden years we'd be talking about the time in college when she picked me up and threw me on her hip, and we'd laugh.

Five months before my wedding, and a week after she and I had a catch-up conversation, I got an email from her. It ended with "I will always have love for you whenever we cross paths. Take really good care of yourself until then, and congratulations on this important next chapter of your life."

She'd ended our almost two-decade-long friendship over email.

You're probably like, "Wait, what happened?" Thanks for asking. I was going to tell you anyway. My husbae and I were having two weddings: a traditional Yoruba ceremony and a Western one (white dress, tux, etc.). The Yoruba ceremony was to honor my lineage (I'm from Nigeria), and it's a colorful celebration where the bride and groom wear traditional outfits in the color of their choice. Also, the couple have an *aso ebi* squad. *Aso ebi* is Yoruba for "clothes of kin," which basically means that people who are in it wear matching clothes. Their fabric tells guests that they are our crew.

As we were planning the wedding, my fiancé and I made a rule that for someone to be in our respective wedding squads, both of us had to have met the person. It meant the friends he chose couldn't be strangers to me, and the friends I chose couldn't be strangers to him. This friend of mine didn't meet this criterion because she actually hadn't met my fiancé in person, even though he and I had been together for four years at that point. I think they might have spoken once on the phone. He didn't even really know her, which in itself was a sign that she and I had drifted apart. Of course she was invited to the wedding. She simply wouldn't be in the squad wearing matching fabric.

The email I received, breaking up our friendship, was in response to that. She assumed that because she wasn't in the squad, our friendship was irrevocably broken. And she saw fit to send me an email ending our seventeen-year relationship.

Reading the email actually gave me a stomachache. Platonic heartbreak is just as real as the romantic kind, and knowing that I'd lost someone whom I considered important to me felt physically painful.

When we tell people that we've lost a friend, we receive platitudes like "Well, some people are just in your life for a season." Or "You will find out who's your real friend. Honor it." Or "Consider yourself lucky to have one less person to deal with who isn't really there for you." Those things can all be true logically, but heart-wise, you might feel like you got hit by a dump truck.

I've been friend-broken-up-with before, but this was the most painful one yet. I remember sitting on my couch that night in tears, feeling insignificant and disposable. My fiancé (now husband) saw how sad I was, and he commented with one of those platitudes: "Honestly, if she didn't make the *aso ebi* squad, it means you weren't as close as you might have thought." He wasn't wrong at all. Yet and still, it hurt like hell.

Why does this loss feel so big? Because oftentimes these are the people you assume will be there come the highs and lows of life. These are the people you think will be your shoulder to lean on if the person you're playing horizontal boogie with decides to dip. It leaves you feeling raw and vulnerable in a real way, because it doesn't feel like a rejection of you as a lover; it feels like a rejection of you as a person.

I retreated from my friends. I didn't do anything major or drastic—I just went into my own bubble. I spoke when spoken to, but I didn't initiate much contact with people. I was deep in my feelings of "if she can do that, anyone can." I was grieving the end of knowing that this person was someone I could call if I needed to, and it showed up as me pulling back from others to try to brace myself against hurt.

But this is where community shows up. This is when I learned what it was like for the village to fill our gaps. This is when my heart was mended.

A couple of months after I received the email, my friend J messaged me to say she knew I would be speaking at a conference in Miami. She told me to give her my schedule while there because she wanted to plan a bachelorette weekend for me. She told me to mind my business and ask no questions, and that she would meet me in Miami the Friday after my talk.

Late Thursday night, J showed up at my hotel room, told me to pack all my things up, and then said, "We're going to the airport. The rule still remains: ask no questions." Thus began the epic saga that was my bride-napping bachelorette trip to Anguilla, where nine of my girlfriends showed up and surprised me.

I was taken from my hotel to the airport, where we boarded a flight to Atlanta, and one friend popped up on that flight. When we landed in ATL, four of my friends were waiting as we exited the plane. There I was blindfolded and walked to another gate, where another friend surprised me. I looked up at the screen near the gate, and it said "St. Maarten." This was where I fell out on the ground. THEY'RE TAKING ME TO ST. MAARTEN??? OMG. But wait, that's out of the country, and I definitely didn't have my passport on me.

Right on cue, J pulled it out of her bag and handed it to me. WHATTT?? My fiancé had mailed her my passport. Because: PREPARED. We boarded the flight, and two more friends were on the plane. I was trapped in a glass case of emotions. It was too much in the BEST of ways.

We took off, ten people strong, and landed in St.

Maarten, where we were led to a boat: our real destination was Anguilla!!! We played loud music and enjoyed the thirty-minute boat ride, with drinks flowing, and I felt my heart growing to three times its usual size.

Once we went ashore I was taken to our home for the next five days: a beautiful beachfront villa at the Four Seasons, with its own private pool. *faints*

Over those five days, we had pajama nights, pool nights, a spa day, and a privately catered dinner. The trip was perfectly curated to make sure that I felt loved and celebrated as I was going into this new season in my life as a wife. They gave me gifts, advice, and time, all while in paradise. My favorite parts of the trip were eating like gluttons, drinking like fish, and laughing like drunk hyenas. We danced so much, played games, and shared heartfelt stories. It was one of the best trips of my life and one of the biggest showings of love I've ever experienced.

It was the salve to my wound.

The last night of the trip, I remember sitting at the head of the table, looking at these nine women who had taken a week out of their lives to shower me with love, and my eyes started leaking. They didn't even know how much this gift meant to me. They didn't know how significant it was to be made to feel so significant. It wasn't even the opulence of it all. It was the time, energy, and presence. Because what they did was pick me up from the depths of self-doubt, anguish, and dejection, and show me affection and tenderness that only your girls know how to snuggle you up in.

And they wanted nothing from me in return. All they wanted was my presence and openness to receiving their love. All they wanted was to see me chase joy and catch it.

That trip changed my life. Not because it was extravagant. Or that we were at the Four Seasons living the life our parents had never even dared to dream up for us. It changed my life because it shifted something in me about what friendship really looks like.

Oftentimes, we get too busy to connect with those we love. But these women stopped their lives for me, and I didn't have the words to express my gratitude. I would have been fine with Miami or ATL or Cleveland or even my living room for that bachelorette celebration, and it would have meant something very similar. But they went above and beyond and took me to paradise in Anguilla. I reveled in all of it because they fed my spirit and my heart. They showed up for me when I really needed it, and showed how much "sisterhood" is a verb.

These two situations, back-to-back, taught me a few key things.

Our feelings are valid, but they aren't permanent. Heartbreak can be painful, but we cannot stay in it. If I had been left to my own devices, I would have continued to wallow. If my other friends hadn't insisted on taking me on that trip, I would have gone from the conference back to my couch, avoiding people and continuing my own retreat of one. Do I still miss this friend from time to time? I do. But the wound the situation left isn't raw anymore and doesn't ache much.

How people react to us is usually about them, not us. This is why we shouldn't constantly internalize the situations we find ourselves in or the treatment we receive. We can absolutely be introspective about what we need to adjust, but we shouldn't use it to create judgments about who we are. I let it make me feel disposable and thought I wasn't worth fighting for or worth giving grace to. But really, maybe this ex-friend of mine was going through a rough time, and maybe she already had another relationship that was fraught, so it made her handle ours the way she did. Maybe it was less about me being a shitty person and more about her not having the capacity to handle it differently.

Friendship is not about transactions. We cannot keep score in friendships, approaching relationships thinking about how we can pay someone back for their acts of kindness. The Bridal Luvv trip was such an amazing time, and I remember thinking, "How can I pay them back?" I cannot. And that's okay. They gave me a gift, and I do not need to feel like I am somehow indebted. I can be appreciative, though. After the trip, I sent them each a package with my favorite skincare products and I wrote each of them a personal note about what their presence meant to me. That's all I could do. Nothing more.

Because friendship isn't about payback or keeping score.

Friendship isn't even in the giant gestures or the big trips. I know my friends and I wouldn't have been able to have that trip five years ago. We JUST got nice things yesterday. To be a friend is to show appreciation, from a well-timed phone call to a lovely note to going over and doing the laundry they haven't had time for. Or taking their kids for the evening so they can go on a date. Great friendships aren't necessarily in the material things; we can show appreciation with gestures that are acts of service.

I reflect on that time and think about the highs and the lows. I think about how my friends knew I was going through a rough time and decided to do something that would be meaningful to me. I think about how I felt too beat up to even fight them on it. It was all a gift. Because it taught me that with the valley of heartbreak, even when platonic, can come some really amazing peaks of community. In the loss I felt from losing that friend, I gained deeper love and companionship in the friends who showed up for me and showed me that my sisterhood is present and strong.

I was reminded that we are always worth loving, and although people might walk away from us, we are always worth cherishing.

THE WISDOM OF A GROUP AND THE WISDOM OF THE SELF

PRIYA PARKER

WHEN I WAS IN HIGH SCHOOL, MY MOM ORGANIZED conversation circles with my friends in our basement on Monday evenings. We would invite a dozen or so girls and sit in a circle on pillows. She would begin by teaching us breathing and meditation exercises, then lead very purposeful discussions in which we explored our identities as young women—who we were, what we stood for. My mother wanted to bring her own experience as an anthropologist to guide us through the anxiety-provoking transitions we found ourselves in. She could have done this just for me, but she knew there was something powerful about doing it in a group.

The group was a mix of brainy-but-irrelevant band nerds like me and popular, cool girls whose sudden presence in our basement came as a shot of adrenaline. One of my friends, Jenna, was a crossover figure in our little school. She was that rare bird who had cachet across social groups, and because *she* thought my mother was "the coolest," twelve very different girls all signed up. In that circle of safety and confidence, we'd discuss all manner of topics: How did we find our voice? Was it okay to admit you wanted something? When should we speak up in class? Did we want to be liked by boys, or was that too terrifying? Do you tell the truth if someone asks you what kind of music you like?

My mother took our teenage issues seriously. She'd take the shame out of an embarrassing issue by bringing it into the open and examining it in a matter-of-fact way. One girl had trouble speaking in public without her voice shaking, and together we all practiced breathing exercises that could help steady our voices. Another shared about the emotional distance she felt from her mother. A few of us had one in common: we were jealous (and admiring) of one of our group members and her seemingly effortless, pixie-like beauty and presence. When we realized others felt it too, we experienced the strange relief of shared confession and came away with a lighter sense of tenderness and affection for this girl, as well as for ourselves. *All these emotions are okay and normal*, my mother seemed to say. And when we named them, together and out loud, their grip loosened.

She wanted us to speak from the heart, so she devised exercises to help us skip to the meaningful while still making it relevant and fun and powerful. One technique was to pair with a partner and stare in her eyes for a full minute. During that exercise, I understood that there were some friends with whom I could do this and others with whom I couldn't because we'd erupt in giggles. My mother would encourage us to delve deeper and ask why we could hold eye contact with some girls and not others. Whom did we feel safe enough to be vulnerable with? Through simple exercises like eye-gazing, she was helping us remove our high school armor of giggling and teasing and deflective jokes, and instead speak honestly about what was happening in our lives. To hold eye contact for so long with someone I knew felt scary. In order to do it, we both had to quiet ourselves and yet be open enough to connect. In my basement, on a circle of pillows on Monday nights, she created a very different way of being together, in front of one another. We called the group Circle of Friends. I came to believe that groups, when structured well, carried wisdom and could solve problems.

My parents hail from very different backgrounds—my mother from Varanasi, an ancient city known as the spiritual capital of India, my father from conservative South Dakotan farmers by way of Iowa. They eventually got divorced, and both went on to remarry, finding spouses more aligned with their worldviews.

After their divorce they had joint custody, so every two weeks I moved between my mother's and father's houses. They lived a mere mile apart, but each household was another universe: my mom's was vegetarian, liberal, Buddhist-Hindu, and wreathed in incense, while my father's was evangelical Christian and solidly Republican. So it was perhaps unsurprising that I ended up in the field of conflict resolution.

Today I am a seasoned professional and master facilitator—someone trained in the skill of shaping group dynamics and collective conversations. As I detail in my book *The Art of Gathering: How We Meet and Why It Matters,* my job is to guide people to collectively think, argue, heal, envision, trust, and connect for a specific larger purpose, just as my mother did so many years earlier. I do this with government officials, business leaders, activists, technology companies, and educators across the world. I help them to understand that in order to come together with their companies or communities in a way that can effect change, they must be clear about their desires and goals. I had become so good at helping others identify their intentions that in my late twenties, I found myself having lost a sense of my own.

From the age of seven or eight, I wanted to be a diplomat. At the University of Virginia, I studied political and social thought and trained to be a conflict resolution facilitator. I spent six years as a facilitator and trainer of facilitators, focusing on race on college campuses and Hindu-Muslim conflict in India. I apprenticed for many years with a senior diplomat and leader in the field of dialogue and conflict transformation. I eventually went on to the Harvard Kennedy School to study public policy. Then came the 2008 financial crisis. I became increasingly convinced that in order to solve complex problems at a sufficiently high level, I needed an MBA to understand markets and business. In my mind, today's diplomats need MBAs. The Kennedy School had a joint business degree program with MIT Sloan. I applied for it with the idea of studying organizational design.

At the Kennedy School, I had been happy. At MIT, I felt like an alien. All the training I had done up to that point no longer seemed relevant. The craft of conflict resolution and facilitation, how to get a group to talk in a way that actually changes something, now seemed incompatible with the assumed values of the business school and the core (implicit) assumptions about what (products and tech!) and who (engineers!) change the world.

My values seemed very different from those of my classmates, too; the implicit assumption in my finance classes, for instance, was that taxes are bad, and therefore we were taught how to minimize them. I'd think back to the social policy I'd studied and wonder, *Why is the core assumption that we are trying to minimize taxes? Why is that the goal? Whom is this serving?* I felt a sense that business school was "routinely blinkered," as one Sloan student, John Benjamin, described it in *The New Republic,* "where the principals' overriding goal—profit maximization—is assumed." Proposals other than what's essentially *more business,* he wrote, are brushed aside. This line of thinking seemed to extend into the school's social culture: what was cool (bigger salaries, the right investors, something called "pitch decks"), what people talked about (their path to IPOing), the trips students would pay to go on ("treks" through Silicon Valley), and the types of jobs coveted (working at McKinsey & Company or Goldman Sachs, Amazon or Google). I felt like a stranger in a strange land.

As the months went on, I became more and more insecure. I was quiet in and out of class, afraid of interacting. I started to feel smaller, insignificant, and eventually even physically weaker. My energy plummeted. One day I was in the bathroom at Sloan and saw what appeared to be a white coin above my forehead. A closer look revealed a circle the size of a quarter where there was no hair. I had developed alopecia, which was soon compounded by other autoimmune problems, such as shingles. I'd go to my classes and leave the building as soon as they were dismissed. I became a studious ghost.

My physical breakdown came to a head when I fainted on a plane back to school after a summer job. When the flight landed in Atlanta, I was taken by ambulance to the emergency room as my heart rate dropped to an alarmingly low number—yet a battery of tests revealed nothing.

Back at school, I saw a doctor who ran additional tests and, perhaps more importantly, listened closely to me. He said something like, "There is nothing wrong with you physically, but the way I would describe what you're going through is that your body has been on a war footing and your army has simply run out of supplies. If you're able, I think you should take the semester off, get right with yourself, and heal."

His words resonated with me. I had been trying so hard to become a "businessperson" (and what I falsely believed that entailed) that my body was giving me distress signals. I made the decision to take a leave of absence and try to "get right with myself." I resolved to stay in Cambridge, but essentially closed the shutters. I had been prepping for interviews with highly coveted management consulting groups, and I requested (and received) permission to postpone the process. I moved into a tiny attic with a roommate and began living simply and cheaply. I tracked my expenses. I cooked a lot of eggs. I took the T everywhere. I emailed close friends and said, "I'm having some scary health issues, and I'm taking some time off. I'm going to be here, but I need some space. I love you." By choosing to press pause on my social life, too, I didn't need money for coffee dates, lunches, or weekend trips, either.

I began to practice getting very, very still.

I had a mentor at the time who told me to practice becoming aware of what I wanted to do in each minute, and then simply to do it—no second-guessing, no self-analysis, no shame or embarrassment or "shoulds." The idea was that (in part because of my childhood, and in part because of my training as a cross-cultural facilitator) I had become so highly attuned to reading the culture I was in that my ability to read myself had atrophied.

During that semester off, I did not set an alarm. I would wake up whenever I woke up and just sit. I wouldn't have a plan, which for someone who had always maintained a full schedule was difficult. Instead, I'd pause. I wouldn't check my phone. I wouldn't jump up and start the day. I'd meditate for a bit. Then I would ask myself: What do I want now?

BEING BIRACIAL, I have spent my life trying to figure out where and to whom I belong. During the tumultuous time when my parents split up, and later being part of two very different families every two weeks, I developed the ability to fit within both families, which were almost polar opposites—Indian British liberals on one side, white Christian conservatives on the other. I could Bollywood dance and I threw a mean softball pitch. I meditated and learned pranic healing, sang Christian pop and led grace. I learned to read a room and grasp very quickly what my mother or father needed.

But I hadn't spent much time isolating and articulating what *I* needed—or, even more radically, what I wanted. "What do I want?" seems a very simple question, but it's weighted and sometimes distorted by cultural expectations, family expectations, and your own carefully cultivated self-image.

And there's a societal belief, particularly for women, who have been socialized to focus on responsibility and the care of others, that it's a bad thing to have a desire—or the word is too narrowly perceived, thought of as a proxy for sexual desire. "Desire" is a much more complicated, robust word. It's difficult to chisel and harness and hone in on what you want. Having hit bottom at Sloan, sitting alone in my attic apartment, I felt a new willingness to try to figure it out.

I started by breaking it down into tiny experiments. How could I know what I wanted to do with my life if I wasn't sure what I wanted to do with my day? Whatever slight desire came up, I would follow it: I'd walk, or do yoga, or cook, or nap, or sit in a café with a book (which I had sometimes imagined myself doing but had never actually done). I also remembered that I'd always loved to dance. Among my happiest childhood moments were the times I'd spent choreographing dances with friends to music by Paula Abdul or Madonna. For me, that was real play. And I loved it.

There is a dance center in Cambridge that I used to pass on my way to class, wondering: *Who is inside? What are they doing right now?* I would look at it longingly, thinking about the lucky people who got to go there. One day during my time off, I walked by it and thought, *I guess I could go there.* This realization was part of a practice of not judging what I actually wanted to do. It is not rocket science. It's simply not ignoring or flicking away the voice in one's head. Without overthinking it, I signed up.

On my first day of class, I felt humbled. I was overwhelmed by the complicated steps. Once we learned the steps, the dances were practiced through organizing ourselves into four lines, then sweeping across the floor in a row, almost like galloping. While waiting, the rest would watch, study, and clap when someone was particularly good. The more talented dancers knew the steps well enough that they could then improvise within the steps. And people celebrated the individual nuance because it signaled how well they had mastered the collective beat.

I didn't know what I was doing as I flailed around. There wasn't grace in my movement. But I kept showing up on Monday nights. Gradually my body began to heal. I was getting ten to twelve hours of sleep a night, and as I rested, I began to wake up earlier. I no longer delayed a meal because I was busy, and (surprise, surprise!) my hands no longer shook from low blood sugar. The slow motion of yoga began to strengthen my muscles. At first the jumps required in dance class freaked me out. I'd jump tentatively. But over time I realized, with relief and surprise, my body could take it. I no longer felt so fragile. I was not particularly skilled, but I loved the freedom of motion, the syncopation, the ability to create something physical together with other people. Studying the syncopation and sequencing of our group dances, I began to see that we were participating in a sophisticated, deliberative, collective method of group intelligence. This is what I'd originally wanted to study at MIT, and I had arrived here via a different route.

And yet, there was still a part of me that raised a note of concern as I walked into that dance complex: *Is this really what I should be spending my time on?* In my mind, that's just not what Serious People did. My regular attendance became a simple act where my beliefs about myself and my interests began to match the way I actually spent my time. I had thought of myself as a dancer, but I hadn't regularly danced since middle school. I had thought of myself as someone who loves to read, but I hadn't read a full book outside of class for years. I kept telling myself, *Ignore your "shoulds." Focus on what you want, and tune out the other noise.*

AS I DANCED and read and rested, I started to feel a new energy and enthusiasm when I thought about work. I reached out to some of my peers, sharing what had really been going on with me, and realized that many of them were also feeling unclear and confused about their sense of purpose—and, like me, having myriad stress-related ailments, from ulcers and alopecia to panic attacks. I was not alone. So I decided to try an experiment.

I began hosting Visioning Labs for groups of friends and peers, not too different from the Circle of Friends sessions of my high school years. I organized the practices and tools I'd learned in my time off into a workshop format where we'd try to get in touch with our truest desires, intentions, and goals. I'd ask participants to think back to moments in which they felt fully alive and to write down, without thinking or judging, all the ways they'd spend a year if they had no fear and no constraints. Through honest sharing and open-minded analysis, we would begin to pinpoint our strengths, interests, and purposes. My hope was that they would leave feeling clearer on their desires, their objectives, their sense of what was worthy in their lives, and what important instincts and dreams they had been ignoring.

By the end of my leave of absence, I no longer felt tired or weak. I continued to be careful with my body, making sure to get at least eight hours of sleep a night, practicing yoga, dancing, and cooking and eating consistent, healthy, simple meals. As I prepared to return to school and work, I wanted to make sure that I didn't forget what I had learned about myself—from the activities I enjoyed in my free time to the kind of work that felt fulfilling and true to my purpose, like the Visioning Labs. I had loved creating these experiences for people who, like me, had lost their way. I bowed out of my pending job interviews. I wanted to be a facilitator—and having fought so hard to find out what I wanted, I never wanted to lose sight of it again.

I spent the next year hosting three Visioning Labs a week in my little shared apartment, aiming to hone my craft, discern patterns, and build a methodology. That year I ran ninety-three of them. Word spread through friends and classmates. I didn't charge; I just wanted to practice. (And it turns out there were a lot of people as lost as I was.) During these discussions, I noticed that most people would cry at some point—not out of sadness, but from hitting some sort of truth. Crying, I realized, could be the release not just of emotions but of information. I began to get notes from friends and friends of friends of friends that the experience had been electrifying, that it had been a "joyful shove" back on their path, or that they were reminded of who they actually were. Perhaps just as meaningful to me was how I continued to feel energized in my daily life. The thought of school and work no longer exhausted me. Staying true to myself had a lasting physical effect— just as *not* staying true to myself had. I continued to sleep well, eat well, dance, and do yoga, too. I understood that doing meaningful work required more than just my mind to be healthy. When I graduated, I committed to going out on my own and launching a business around facilitation and vision.

The Visioning Labs were built around a core question that I worked on and worked on and worked on, and still believe is one of the most powerful questions one can ask: What is the biggest need in the world that you might have the passion and capacity to address? Since that can be a daunting question to answer, I'd walk people through it, breaking it down into smaller questions, like: What is an early experience you had that connects you with the work you do today? If you had a year of your life that you could spend in any way and money wasn't an issue, how would you spend it? I'd listen and reflect back to participants what I saw in what they wrote, drew, and shared. In the meantime, I continued to pursue dance and eventually enrolled in a two-hundred-hour yoga dance teacher training. I did each thing slowly and at my own pace. Each time I thought about adding or removing an activity from my life, I'd pause and check in with myself, asking: *Is this what I want?* And I stopped judging which piece of my life was "serious enough" to inform my work.

Years later, as I have brought together my training in group dialogue, conflict resolution, identity studies, marching band, voice dialogue, yoga dance training, multi-stakeholder deliberation studies, and, yes, those trips to the dance complex, I began to realize that they all deeply inform my practice. Today, what I do in my personal life and what I choose to focus on in my work is a mix of the many decisions I've made—many that didn't make sense at the time—to follow my interests and my instincts.

And the thread that I try to bring to all my work— whether with political activists or multi-generational families or complicated group partnerships—ties back to that dancing and even to my mother's circles: you are among others, but you are seen for who you are.

ON SILENCE

NATALIE GUERRERO

I'VE HAD A FEW BROKEN HEARTS IN MY LIFE. SOME big, some small, but none as massive as those that were self-made. None as impactful as those I married to my silence. None as harsh and as tender as those I swallowed down, never let breathe, or adamantly shielded from the light of day.

A few years back, after I learned the hard way that first love doesn't always last forever, my heartbreak took the shape of a plane ticket to Paris. Can you imagine? 3,367 miles all just to get away from myself.

I had been dying to visit Shakespeare and Co., the renowned bookstore in the heart of the city. So one Friday morning, I picked my sorry self up and ventured out. As I scanned the shelves for something that screamed UNBREAK MY HEART, my eyes met a tiny pink paperback. The words on the cover were deliberate. Focused. And speaking straight to me. In big white letters I read, AUDRE LORDE. And then—YOUR SILENCE WILL NOT PROTECT YOU.

I stopped dead in my tracks. That can't be right, I thought. My silence is the only thing that has ever protected me. And then I felt my stomach flip a little bit. Like something inside me wasn't so sure that was true.

Was I wrong? Had my silence been the breeding ground for the ways my heart was breaking? Was it doing more suffocating than serving? And if my silence wasn't protecting me, what was?

Before I knew it, I was sitting upstairs on a green cushioned stool, the store cat next to me, devouring Audre's words for the first time. My heart was beating fast. It was like looking in a mirror, seeing all the words I never gave myself permission to say. It was like finding a road map. One that I'd been searching years for. One that actually seemed to belong to me, instead of the great big world outside myself.

Maybe Paris was working, I thought. Maybe I had escaped all the ways I was swallowing myself whole. Maybe I was done with the small game. Maybe, I thought, today was the first day of the rest of my life.

By the end of the night, I decided there was a God. And her name was Audre Lorde.

On the plane ride home, in a game I've since named Audre Lorde Meets Life, I made a list of a few times I had been silent. It read:

1. Yesterday, when I wanted red wine but the waiter had already opened the white.
2. Freshman year, when I swore nothing bad happened to me in that frat basement.
3. Last April, when my boss told me I had only been hired because I was "skinny and pretty."
4. On the playground in fifth grade when a boy named Bobby called me a n*gger.
5. On the Metro-North from Larchmont to New York City, when I fainted instead of saying I was too hot and needed to sit down.

God, it was starting to feel like I had spent my entire life in the quiet car.

I read this list over and over for what must have been the entire nine hours to New York. I looked at myself on that piece of paper with fear, a little bit of empathy, and a whole lot of commitment to stop behaving like my silence would protect me. What struck me most about this list was the way my silence didn't pick and choose only small moments to show itself. Instead, it reared its head no matter where I went. It was ever present no matter what the stakes were. Silence, I came to discover, was my master. And I had been waiting on it hand and foot for fear that the alternative would be crueler. If I let it continue, I realized, that same silence would sabotage me.

When I got back to New York I felt fine for the first few days—that magic dust from Paris was still all over me. I felt it at the coffee shop, when the barista handed me an almond milk latte and I quickly said, "Excuse me, but I ordered oat milk." She looked at me, offended, and as she dumped my coffee down the drain, I heard her murmur, "Or you could just drink it." But that was exactly it—I *couldn't*. I had decided to stop drinking down whatever life served up for me. And isn't it funny how the world finds us to be so unpalatable when we start to ask for the things we actually want?

Eventually, though, that new-car smell started wearing off. It was slow at first. I'd find myself sharing a meal when I wanted my own, saying I was full when I hadn't eaten a thing all day, going to the bar when what I really needed was a face mask and a night in. And then, suddenly, the silence was seeping into every big corner of my life. I fell back into relationships I'd sworn off. I made no time for myself. I worked until I could barely see my computer screen. When I woke up in the morning, my hands would be shaking, screaming at me to slow down, but instead I simply put them to work. I started doing everything I could to look away from myself. I volunteered, took on extra work, took weekend trips in an attempt to escape the sinking feeling I had every day. It never worked, but I posted about those trips on Instagram as if it did. But what I was really doing was letting go of Audre Lorde's godly pages and slipping back into my smallness. Being small was comfortable enough in its familiarity to create a feeling of safety, of power even. But I could never surprise myself. I knew everything in this version of my life. I could predict every outcome, and here's how it would go:

I never ask for anything, so I never hurt.
I say "I love you" because it's the polite thing to do.
I marry the boy.
I drink coffee in the morning.
I drink beer at night.
I have three or five kids.
I'm successful, whatever that means.
I never say no.
I learn how to ski.
I am grateful.
But I am not content.

So there I was again, staying safe, saying yes when I meant to say no, saying no when I meant to say yes, showing up for everyone but myself. I was choosing what felt comfortable and familiar over what felt true and terrifying. There was a voice inside of me screaming for change, but I committed myself to pushing it down, smothering it with my need for control.

And so for the next year, I stayed silent. I watched my life like it was a movie. All the while, I wondered if I'd missed my one great big chance to live my life the way I wanted. I wondered if I had missed the boat and now it was too late. I kept thinking about Shakespeare and Co.—the way I'd lit up and seen glimpses of a life I could be proud of, a parallel universe where I never backed down. Where I was relentless in the pursuit of my own liberation. I kept thinking about the way I'd sat down and written away my silence on that airplane. How certain I'd felt that things would be different by now—that I would be better by now. I kept asking myself, how did I end up here . . . again? That's when the shame crept in. And that's when I sank further into my silence. It turns out that my shame and my silence were great partners in me staying stuck.

So every day when I woke up and stepped willfully into my smallness, I also wondered how I could reclaim that feeling—the one I'd been so sure of when I left Paris. And not only that, but how I could move from having the feeling to acting on it? I clung to one thing: I believed in Audre's words to my bones. I knew that my silence wouldn't protect me, but I didn't know how I could break that silence. My knowing was not enough to change my behavior. Instead, it seemed only to fuel my shame and, in turn, my silence.

Then, one morning, I was walking in midtown Manhattan when I heard a couple fighting on the sidewalk. She was screaming and he was red in the face. Finally she stopped yelling, and then, faintly, I heard her say, "You never choose me." I scoffed. There was something about the way she was begging him for acceptance that sat cold in my belly. And I thought, *Sister, choose yourself.* I looked at her, and then in her eyes I saw myself. She was me, holding her arms open, waiting to be chosen, giving up all her power until she was given permission to take it back. So now *I* stopped. And I thought again, this time telling myself, *Sister, choose yourself.* It turns out that I had been confused this whole time. I was telling myself that Paris was my permission. That I had lost it. But in this electric moment, I realized: What if I am my own? What if I belong to myself? What if the road map is not something to be found in a bookstore three thousand miles away? What if the road map is already within me? What if I stop running from myself and start running TO myself?

I started by asking myself: What can I do TODAY that will help me tomorrow? I left the relationships I had let fester, speaking the words I had swallowed down. I made the move across the country that I had always wanted to do. I cut out making plans with people who left me feeling alone even when we were to-gether. Most importantly, I started speaking up when I saw something happen out in the world that didn't sit well with me. It was really hard, all the unlearning. It was painful, and I lost people and I let people down. Sometimes I felt so alone that I started to question all the steps I'd taken. But I also began to learn that my answer is always somewhere in my voice. It might be unsure, or shaky, or half-baked, but now when I ques-tion myself, my voice is the thing that I turn to—not my silence. I had waited patiently for a God. Then I found Audre. Now it was finally time to trust my own mind to point me in the next direction.

Around the time I started to disown my silence, I took up running. I thought instead of running from my fears, I'd actually let my feet hit the pavement. My morning runs became the times I got most honest with myself. I can hear myself on a run. I can separate out the silences from the truth. I can ask myself big questions, like what I want from the world and what I think I can give back to it.

One morning last May I was visiting my family in my lily-white picket-fenced hometown and I went out on my morning run. I wanted to gain some clarity in this place that had both bred me and beaten me down. After all, this was the place I learned my silence. I learned here first what it meant to be Black. Silence in this town was a defense mechanism. I used it to hide away from my skin and my hair and all the things that made me special and stick out like a sore thumb. I learned to shrink in the hope that no one would notice I was different.

In between all the big thoughts filling my brain while I ran, I counted the mansions I passed, panting. Most importantly, I made sure to smile. When you're Black in a white neighborhood, you have to smile. For some reason, on this particular day, I was painfully aware of it.

When I got home, I heard Ahmaud Arbery's name for the first time. Here's what I learned: On February 23, 2020, Ahmaud Arbery was enjoying a nice run on a beautiful day, just like I had that morning. Ahmaud began to be stalked by two armed men. They cornered him. Shot him three times, eventually killing him, and then, as he was bleeding out, they turned him over to see if he was armed. After that they went home and stayed there for months.

Ahmaud died alone and in the street. Disposed of like a piece of roadkill. Ahmaud's life was individual. It will never be replicated, or returned to us, or given the chance to become. And yet I knew that, in all his brilliant singularity, Ahmaud Arbery was me—counting mansions in a lily-white town. He was sporting my same skin, letting his feet hit the pavement, and I wondered if he too knew he had to smile.

From that moment on, it seemed selfish to focus

only on dismantling my own personal silence. I had to take it a step further. I had to dismantle the way the world revolved in silence. So I thought, What is it about silence that lures us in so insidiously? How is silence making the world sick? How can we defeat it? And what part have I played in maintaining it?

And then there I was, thinking about Audre Lorde again. This time, though, I was thinking about how many ways we as Black people have been taught to stay silent. We have internalized all the same lessons I myself had fought to overcome. We've been taught to stay small in order to stay safe. To put our hands up and be still. Never to talk back. Never to look up. Never to make a sudden movement for fear it might be our last. To become invisible. To straighten our spine. Work twice as hard. Lower the volume. In short, we have been taught that our silence will protect us.

And that's when I saw our nation like I saw myself: unraveling from a lifetime of looking away, and paying the price for all the ways we've been stuck in our silence. While my Black peers' silence felt rooted in fear for their lives, the white silence I witnessed seemed to be rooted in fear of losing their power. It was that white silence that kept harmful systems alive. It was white silence that stood in the way of change.

In the next few weeks I felt myself boiling, all the time. I was calling my representatives, but I was also in the grocery store ripping through the shelves, outraged that they were out of my favorite cereal. I was stepping into my power, raising thousands of dollars in donations, but I was also at the airport seething because my flight was delayed an hour. I was writing, speaking more than I ever had, interviewing victims of police brutality, and posting all my words on the internet. I was also at the dinner table ready for war because my brother took what I considered to be my seat. I was a storm of emotions, and working on balance felt a bit like walking a tightrope. I was standing in front of all my fury and searching for a productive place to put it.

Here's what I didn't know about silence until I popped the lid open: once you're through with it, years of unexpressed rage bubble to the surface. Audre Lorde also says, "Women responding to racism is women responding to anger." I would like to add that our response often sounds a lot like the screams of our caged voices finally being set free.

The subtext of my anger, as well as our nation's, had everything to do with how comfortable we'd been in silence and how we were willingly letting our souls rot from the inside out. While I was outraged, I was asking, How much time have I lost because of my silence? At the same time, the nation was asking, How much blood is on our hands because of our silence? The answer was the same: too much.

I never knew how addicting it could be to stay small until I saw a glimpse of being bigger. I saw the way I buried myself in my smallness, and once I named that smallness, I saw how sick the world was with it too. At some point we have all succumbed to staying stuck. We have all succumbed to silence. America's silence is the same soul sickness that lived inside me for years.

So when I look at who we are as a nation, I think about both my heartbreak and my silence. I think about the ways I swallowed it down, and then I think about the ways the United States has done that too. Then I think, *Sister, CHOOSE yourself.* It is our turn to find the road map home that lives within the soul of this place. We are the answer that we have been looking for—we just have to stop asking for permission to get there. We have to ask ourselves what we can do TODAY that will help us tomorrow. We have to break our silence—first inside our own lives, and then outside of them too. It may not inoculate us from heartbreak, but it will protect us from betraying ourselves. Because the only thing I'm sure of now is that when we break our silence and speak our truth, we don't only free ourselves. We free the world.

EPILOGUE

JENNIFER RUDOLPH WALSH

MAYA ANGELOU'S WORDS WERE MY FIRST INTRODUC-
tion to the transformational power of storytelling.
Though I belonged to a different generation and race,
hadn't grown up impoverished or in the South, and
hadn't spent years mute (in fact, I couldn't stop talking), it still felt to me that Maya Angelou was somehow
telling my story—a young woman's longing to be seen
and heard. To believe that despite her pain, she was
still worthy of love and her life mattered.

As she wrote in *I Know Why the Caged Bird Sings,*
"There is no greater agony than bearing an untold
story inside you." This simple, powerful truth unites
all the stories in this collection, from Nkosi Mabaso's
resilience after trauma and Austin Channing Brown's
deep-seated fear of ambition to Cameron Esposito's

lonely path toward belonging and Jillian Mercado's refusal to be treated with anything less than respect. Each one of these fierce storytellers creates a beautiful mosaic of lived experiences. Despite our differences, we can find part of ourselves in each. Most importantly, we need both sides of storytelling—listening to others' stories and telling our own—to embrace one another in our full humanity. In bearing witness, we allow ourselves to be witnessed. This is the life-changing power of storytelling—to connect those of us who will never meet or have just met, as well as to deepen our connections to the people we love the most. Listen with an open heart and without judgment to what others have to share, and take courage from these pages as you go out and tell the world your truth. Magic is waiting for you.

ACKNOWLEDGMENTS

FIRST AND FOREMOST, MY DEEPEST GRATITUDE TO MY partner-in-creation of Together Live, the untamed Glennon Doyle, along with all the fierce speakers who blessed my life and our stage with their stories: Abby Wambach, Alicia Keys, Alisa Roadcup, Amanda Gorman, Amani Al-Khatahtbeh, Amena Brown, Ashley C. Ford, Austin Channing Brown, Becca Stevens, Bozoma Saint John, Brené Brown, Brittany Packnett Cunningham, Cam, Cameron Esposito, Cheryl Strayed, Ciara, Cleo Wade, Connie Lim aka MILCK, Dr. Knatokie Ford, Elizabeth Lesser, Ella Vos, Geena Rocero, Gina Rodriguez Halima Aden, Ibtihaj Muhammad, Isra Hirsi, Jamia Wilson, Jaycee Gossett, Jen Hatmaker, Jillian Mercado, Kelly Corrigan, Khalida Brohi, Krista Tippett, Latham Thomas, Liliane Kamikazi, Luvvie

Ajayi Jones, Maysoon Zayid, Maytha Alhassen, Melissa Villaseñor, Meredith Walker, Michelle Buteau, Nadia Bolz-Weber, Naomi Ekperigin, Nicole Byer, Nkosi Mabaso, Noor Tagouri, Patti Harrison, Priya Parker, Reese Witherspoon, Resistance Revival Chorus, Reverend Jacqui Lewis, Ruthie Lindsey, Ryan Weiss, Sabrina Jalees, Seane Corn, Sheri Salata, Sonequa Martin Green, Sonia Denis, Sophia Bush, Sue Bird, The War and Treaty (Michael Trotter Jr. and Tanya Blount-Trotter), Uma Thurman, Valarie Kaur, and Yara Shahidi. I am cheering my head off for you always.

A wholehearted thank-you to all the amazing humans who live at the intersection of love and work, and who gave their all to make our traveling love rally and this collection a reality: Brandon Biney, Gina Centrello, Amy Chandy, Donna Cheng, Brittney Duke, Tracy Fisher, Whitney Frick, Kim Fusaro, Suzanne Gluck, Ayelet Gruenspecht, Natalie Guerrero, Sarah Harden, Michelle Jasmine, Patty Kerr, Jason Lublin, Jay Mandel, Caitlin Moore, Elsie Morale, Emilio Pardo, Marc Pritchard, Margaret Riley King, Pepper Schwartz, Maggie Shapiro, Eric Simonoff, Sabrina Taitz, Allison Tummon, Michelle Walter, and especially our editor, Katy Nishimoto, with all the many hats she wore through the years. Teamwork really did make the dream work.

I am forever indebted to my sister/friend Arianna Huffington, who dragged me kicking and screaming onto the stage for the first time, and to Oprah Winfrey, for igniting my mad burning love for live events and showing me the beauty and intimacy of thousands of hearts beating together as one.

Finally, to my devoted family, who cheered me on as I overcame stage fright, packed my carry-on bag year after year, and traveled from town to town: Seeing your smiling faces in the audience along the road always made me feel like I was home. Your love makes me brave.

ABOUT THE CONTRIBUTORS

JENNIFER RUDOLPH WALSH has sat at the nexus of entertainment and media for nearly thirty years. She was WME's sole female board member and global head of its literary, lectures, and conference divisions, and she represented such luminous clients as Oprah Winfrey, Brené Brown, Alice Munro, and Sue Monk Kidd. In 2016, she co-founded Together Live, a traveling intersectional women's tour driven by the mission of finding purpose and community through authentic and heartfelt storytelling. Over four years, the tour visited thirty-five cities, lit more than fifty thousand souls on fire, and produced three seasons of a widely streamed podcast. She serves as a board advisor to SeeHer, the National Book Foundation, and her alma mater, Kenyon College. After a lifetime in New York City, Jennifer relocated to San Francisco to walk beneath the redwoods with her family and three dogs.

LUVVIE AJAYI JONES, a sought-after speaker who thrives at the intersection of culture, comedy, and justice, is the *New York Times* bestselling author of *I'm Judging You: The Do-Better Manual* and *Professional Troublemaker: The Fear-Fighter Manual*. The inspiration for *Professional Troublemaker* came from her wildly popular TED Talk, which has been viewed more than five million times. A seventeen-year blogging veteran, Luvvie writes on her site, AwesomelyLuvvie.com, covering all things culture with a critical yet humorous lens. She is host of the *Rants & Randomness* podcast and runs a social network called LuvvNation.

Luvvie was chosen by Oprah Winfrey as part of her inaugural SuperSoul100 list, honored with the Outstanding Young Alumni Award by her alma mater, the University of Illinois at Urbana-Champaign, and awarded the Breakthrough Award by the Council of Urban Professionals. Ajayi Jones's work has been featured in outlets such as *The New York Times,* NPR, *Forbes, Inc., Fortune, Essence,* the *Chicago Tribune,* and more. Born in Nigeria, bred in Chicago, and comfortable everywhere, Luvvie is clear that her love language is shoes.

AMENA BROWN is a spoken word poet, author, and performing artist whose work interweaves keep-it-real storytelling, rhyme, and humor. Through her weekly podcast, *HER with Amena Brown,* Amena centers and elevates the voices, stories, and experiences of Black, Indigenous, Asian, and Latinx women. She wrote and collaborated with award-winning actress, producer, and activist Tracee Ellis Ross as the poetic partner for Ross's natural hair care line, PATTERN Beauty. Amena takes arenas, theaters, and performance venues and turns them into living rooms, where performance becomes conversation and builds community. She lives in Atlanta, Georgia, with her husband, DJ Opdiggy.

AUSTIN CHANNING BROWN is a writer, speaker, and media producer providing inspired leadership on racial justice in America. She is the *New York Times* bestselling author of *I'm Still Here: Black Dignity in a World Made for Whiteness* and the executive producer of the web series *The Next Question.*

CAMERON ESPOSITO is a Los Angeles–based comic, actor, and bestselling author. Cameron's career has spanned everything from big-budget films to Sundance indies to animation. She co-starred in and co-created the much-lauded *Take My Wife,* now on Starz, has written for *The New York Times,* and has appeared as herself on TV, on podcasts, and in web series alike. Cameron hosts a popular interview podcast, *Queery with Cameron Esposito,* and her recent hit comedy special, *Rape Jokes,* raised almost $100,000 for rape crisis intervention. Her first book, *Save Yourself,* was released during the pandemic and was still a bestseller. Go, Cam!

ASHLEY C. FORD is a writer, host, and educator who lives in Brooklyn by way of Indiana. Her forthcoming memoir, *Somebody's Daughter,* will be published by Flatiron Books under the imprint An Oprah Book.

Ford is the writer and host of *The Chronicles of Now* podcast. She has written or guest-edited for *The Guardian, ELLE, BuzzFeed, OUT Magazine, Slate, Teen Vogue, New York Magazine, Allure, Marie Claire, The New York Times, Netflix Queue, Cup of Jo,* and various other web and print publications. She's taught creative nonfiction writing at the New School and Catapult.Co, and had her work listed among Longform & Longread's Best of 2017.

NATALIE GUERRERO is a writer and activist from New York who currently resides in Los Angeles, California. All her work, written or otherwise, aims to uplift people of color through highlighting their humanity. She works in film development at MACRO, a POC-run production company whose mission is much like her own, and she is the co-founder of Know My Story, a digital movement on a mission to share true stories from Black people and intersectional voices.

SUE MONK KIDD's debut novel, *The Secret Life of Bees,* spent more than one hundred weeks on the *New York Times* bestseller list, has sold more than six million copies in the United States, was turned into both an award-winning major motion picture and a musical, and has been translated into thirty-six languages. Her second novel, *The Mermaid Chair,* was a number one *New York Times* bestseller and was adapted into a television movie. Her third novel, *The Invention of Wings,* an Oprah's Book Club 2.0 pick, was also a number one *New York Times* bestseller. *The Book of Longings,* her fourth novel, was published to rave reviews and spent weeks on the *New York Times* bestseller list. She is the author of several acclaimed memoirs, including *The Dance of the Dissident Daughter,* her groundbreaking work on religion and feminism, as well as the *New York Times* bestseller *Traveling with Pomegranates,* written with her daughter, Ann Kidd Taylor. She lives in North Carolina.

CONNIE LIM AKA MILCK is a recording artist who performs under the moniker MILCK. In 2017, her song "(I Can't Keep) Quiet"—her reclamation of her voice from sexism, racism, and abuse—became the unofficial global anthem for the Women's March movement and was listed as the number one protest song of the year by *Billboard*. MILCK had the honor of performing "Quiet" at the ESPYs as survivors of Larry Nassar walked the stage to receive the Arthur Ashe Courage Award, a moment that aligned with Connie's belief that inner healing can ripple out to global healing. As a way to express gratitude for the blessing of being able to create music, she created the #ICANTKEEPQUIET Fund and the Somebody's Beloved Fund.

In 2020 MILCK released her second EP, *Into Gold*, executive-produced by Malay, as an ode to the journey of going from survivor to thriver, with *Time* magazine listing her leading single "If I Ruled the World" as song of the week. She continues to share her songs and speeches about finding one's voice onstage with the likes of Yoko Ono, Michelle Obama, Oprah, Cheryl Strayed, Glennon Doyle, Michelle Williams, Dionne Warwick, Jason Mraz, and Ani DiFranco.

NKOSINGIPHILE MABASO is a singer, songwriter, and storyteller who was born and raised in a township called Thokoza in the east of Johannesburg, South Africa. When she was twelve years old, she began attending the Oprah Winfrey Leadership Academy for Girls in South Africa, after which she attended Skidmore College in New York, graduating with honors in sociology. Nkosi is passionate about telling and sharing stories of hope, healing, triumph, and love. As part of the national Together Live tour, she spoke about overcoming challenges that threatened to thwart her progress and how perseverance and love aided her in overcoming those challenges. She is currently in South Africa writing and making music, continuing in her journey to become the woman she wants to be in the world.

JILLIAN MERCADO is a physically disabled Latinx model, an actress, and an advocate for greater representation in the fashion industry. She has appeared in campaigns for Nordstrom, Target, and Olay and on the cover of the first digital September issue of *Teen Vogue*. Her activism, which focuses on the intersection of gender and disability, has included working with UN secretary-general António Guterres in 2018 to reduce inequality, one of the UN's seventeen Sustainable Development Goals. She can currently be seen in a recurring role on the Showtime series *The L Word: Generation Q* opposite Jennifer Beals.

PRIYA PARKER is helping us take a deeper look at how anyone can create collective meaning in modern life, one gathering at a time. She is a master facilitator, strategic advisor, acclaimed author of *The Art of Gathering: How We Meet and Why It Matters*, and the host and executive producer of the *New York Times* podcast *Together*

Apart. Trained in the field of conflict resolution, Parker has worked on race relations on American college campuses and on peace processes in the Arab world, southern Africa, and India. Parker is a founding member of the Sustained Dialogue Campus Network, a member of the World Economic Forum Global Agenda Council on New Models of Leadership, and a senior expert at Mobius Executive Leadership. She studied organizational design at MIT, public policy at the Harvard Kennedy School, and political and social thought at the University of Virginia. She has spoken on the TED Main Stage, and her talks have been viewed more than three million times. She lives with her husband and two children in Brooklyn, New York.

Born and raised in the Philippines, GEENA ROCERO is an award-winning producer, model, public speaker, trans rights advocate, and television host.

On March 31, 2014, in honor of International Transgender Day of Visibility, Rocero came out as transgender at the annual TED Conference. Her viral talk has since been viewed more than four million times and translated into thirty-two languages.

Named a "Top 25 Transgender Person Who Influences Culture" by *Time* magazine, Geena made history as the first trans woman 2020 *Playboy* Playmate of the Year, and again as the first trans woman ambassador for Miss Universe Nepal. She was featured on E's *I Am*

Cait and has been on the cover of *Candy* magazine and in the *Vanity Fair: Trans America* special issue, Marriott's #LoveTravels campaign, and CoverGirl Cosmetics's #GirlsCan campaign.

Geena has spoken at the White House, the World Economic Forum, the United Nations, the State Department, and multiple Fortune 500 companies. She is the founder of Gender Proud, a media production company that tells stories about what it means to be trans and gender nonconforming.

BOZOMA SAINT JOHN is the global chief marketing officer at Netflix, the world's leading streaming entertainment service, with 183 million paid memberships in more than 190 countries enjoying TV series, documentaries, and feature films across a wide variety of genres and languages. Before joining Netflix, Saint John served in executive roles at Endeavor, Uber, Apple Music and iTunes, and PepsiCo. Bozoma has been inducted into *Billboard*'s Women in Music Hall of Fame (2018) and the American Advertising Federation Hall of Achievement (2014), and has been included in the *Hollywood Reporter*'s Women in Entertainment Power 100 list (2018) and *Forbes*'s The World's Most Influential CMOs list (2018).

TANYA BLOUNT-TROTTER was born and raised in Washington, D.C. She attended Morgan State University, where she studied psychology while singing in the university choir. Tanya then continued with a career in both film and music; some notable works include her role in *Sister Act 2: Back in the Habit* and her debut album *Natural Thing*, which charted in the top 100 on R&B/hip-hop albums charts. After retiring from her solo career, she met her now husband, Michael Trotter Jr., in 2010 after she heard him perform at the aptly titled Love Festival. Drawn by the depth and honesty in his songs, she ran across the field in high heels after his set and asked if he ever collaborated with other artists. In storybook fashion, they fell in love, got married, and three years later formed the band The War and Treaty.

MICHAEL TROTTER JR. was born in Cleveland, Ohio, and raised in Washington, D.C. At nineteen years old, Trotter joined the U.S. Army and was stationed in one of Saddam Hussein's palaces in Iraq, where he taught himself how to write songs and play piano on one of Saddam's pianos. After completing two tours, Trotter returned to the United States for good, where he struggled with PTSD and homelessness. A few years later, in an almost cinematic twist, he met his now wife and musical partner, Tanya Blount, at the Love Festival in Maryland. They quickly discovered the magic of their two voices and formed their current band, The War and Treaty.

MAYSOON ZAYID is an actress, comedian, writer, and disability advocate. She is a graduate of and a guest comedian in residence at Arizona State University. Maysoon is the co-founder/co-executive producer of the New York Arab American Comedy Festival and the Muslim Funny Fest. She was a full-time on-air contributor to *Countdown with Keith Olbermann* and is a guest writer for *Vice*. She has most recently appeared on CNN's *New Day, 60 Minutes,* and ABC News. Maysoon had the most viewed TED Talk of 2014 and was named one of 100 Women of 2015 by the BBC.

As a professional comedian, she has performed in top New York clubs and has toured extensively at home and abroad. Maysoon was a headliner on the Arabs Gone Wild Comedy tour and the Muslims Are Coming tour. She appeared alongside Adam Sandler in *You Don't Mess with the Zohan* and is a recurring character on *General Hospital*. Maysoon limped in New York Fashion Week and is the host of the web series *Advice You Don't Want to Hear*. She is the author of the best-selling memoir *Find Another Dream,* and is the creator of the Book of Bay Ann children's graphic novel series.

ABOUT THE TYPE

This book was set in Legacy, a typeface family designed by Ronald Arnholm (b. 1939) and issued in digital form by ITC in 1992. Both its serifed and unserifed versions are based on an original type created by the French punchcutter Nicholas Jenson in the late fifteenth century. While Legacy tends to differ from Jenson's original in its proportions, it maintains much of the latter's characteristic modulations in stroke.